Why You?

CV Messages To Win Jobs

John Lees

The **McGraw·Hill** Companies

London • Burr Ridge IL • New York • St Louis • San Francisco • Auckland • Bogotá • Caracas • Lisbon • Madrid • Mexico • Milan

Montreal • New Delhi • Panama • Paris • San Juan • São Paulo

Singapore • Sydney • Tokyo • Toronto

Why You? CV Messages To Win Jobs
John Lees
ISBN-13 9780077115104
ISBN-10 0077115104

 **Professional**

Published by McGraw-Hill Education
Shoppenhangers Road
Maidenhead
Berkshire
SL6 2QL
Telephone: 44 (0) 1628 502 500
Fax: 44 (0) 1628 770 224
Website: www.mcgraw-hill.co.uk

British Library Cataloguing in Publication Data
A catalogue record for this book is available from the British Library

Library of Congress Cataloging in Publication Data
The Library of Congress data for this book has been applied for from the Library of Congress

Commissioning Editor: Julia Scott
Production Editor: Jonathan Lee
Text design by Robert Gray
Cover design by Jan Marshall
Typeset by Gray Publishing, Tunbridge Wells, Kent
Printed and bound in Great Britain by Bell & Bain

ISBN-13 9780077115104
ISBN-10 0077115104

Contents

PART 3   Making Your CV Work For You

About the Author

John Lees is one of the UK's best-known career coaches. *How To Get A Job You'll Love*, now in its fourth edition, was WH Smith's Business Book of the Month in January 2003, and remains one of the best-selling careers books by a British author.

As a career transition coach, John specialises in helping people make difficult career decisions – either difficult because they don't know what to do next or because there are barriers in the way to success. He has delivered career workshops throughout the UK and, also, in the USA and South Africa, and regularly speaks at UK events (Total Jobs Live, Next Steps, One Life Live) and has featured as a speaker at the world's largest international career conferences in the USA.

He writes regularly for *The Times*, *The Guardian* and *People Management*, and his work has been featured on TV (he was a presenter on the BBC Interactive "Back to Work" programme), widely on radio and in many publications including *Management Today*, *Cosmopolitan*, *Daily Express*, *Daily Mirror*, *Real World*, *Financial World*, *Pathfinder*, *Eve* and *She*. He writes a regular careers column for *Personnel Today*.

A graduate of the universities of Cambridge, London and Liverpool, John has spent most of his career focusing on the world of work. He was formerly Chief Executive of the Institute of Employment Consultants (now the Recruitment & Employment Confederation, REC). He is retained as Senior Associate to outplacement specialists Career Management Consultants Ltd (CMC), and a member of the International Advisory Board of the Association of Career Professionals International (ACPi). John Lees Associates, based in Cheshire, provides help for career changers across the UK.

In addition to his careers work John is an ordained Anglican priest. He works as volunteer clergy in the Diocese of Chester and, as Assistant

Diocesan Director of Ordinands, helps individuals who are considering different kinds of ministry. John lives and works in Cheshire, with his wife, the children's writer, Jan Dean, and their two sons.

For a range of free careers tools, checklists and details of workshops and 1:1 coaching from John Lees Associates see www.johnleescareers.com or telephone 01565 631625.

Other careers books by John Lees published by McGraw-Hill Professional

(see www.jobyoulove.co.uk)

How To Get A Job You'll Love (2007), £12.99
ISBN 13: 9780077114718

Take Control of Your Career (2006), £12.99
ISBN 13: 9780077109677

Job Interviews: Top Answers to Tough Questions (2004), £8.99
ISBN 13: 9780077107048

Acknowledgements

My gratitude goes to all those who have fired ideas, inspiration and encouragement in my direction while writing this book. I would like to thank Kate Berge, Gill Best, Ron Feasey, Jeff Grout, Linda Clark and Joëlle Warren for their very helpful perspectives. I owe a huge debt to Kate Howlett for her advice about layout and eye flow, and Stuart McIntosh of Career Management Consultants Ltd (CMC) for many conversations and for reviewing the manuscript at a key stage in its development.

My particular thanks to Robin Wood, MD of CMC, for his assistance with the CV survey, to his colleague Francis Mulhern for processing the results and to Dominic Box of WebTek for making it all work.

My immense gratitude goes to my editor Julia Scott at McGraw-Hill for encouraging the project and cheering it through to the finish line. Particular thanks to Richard and Sue Doggett, who lent me their Devon cottage to write the first half. And, as ever, to Sue Blake, who continues to prove herself quite possibly the best publicist on the planet.

This book is dedicated to my son Matthew Lees, recently graduated, who never ceases to be a surprise and a blessing.

Preface

"The most important thing in communication is to hear what isn't being said."

Peter Drucker

Every day thousands of hopefuls send off badly composed CVs in pursuit of jobs they don't understand. Even the better CVs do not get shortlisted because they fail to communicate the right message.

As soon as you communicate any kind of message to a decision maker, you open up a set of expectations, questions and doubts. While you might secretly enjoy the idea of being a complex individual, asking just a few questions of recruiters or successful job hunters will show you one important fact: your CV message needs to be clear, uncomplicated and something that prompts the reader to do something – to shortlist you, to see you, to recommend you.

I spend most of my time as a career coach helping people to work on their message. I've also spent over 20 years training recruiters in the art of staff selection and interviewing, which gives me some insights into the way recruiters read you and the (sadly) rather rapid way they read CVs. Most recruiters are conservative – not by disposition, but simply because they are busy people trying to fill a vacancy as efficiently as possible. You may find your "chequered" career interesting, you may feel that your interests are unique and your qualifications are outstanding. Recruiters are more interested in whether you are worth investing time and money in as a potential candidate.

There are many sources of CV advice in the marketplace, so why another CV book? Having helped hundreds of career changers and seen thousands of CVs, and having worked closely with recruiters and HR specialists throughout my career, the evidence suggests that there are still too many people who don't really have an answer to the question "why you?" – in their CV, in their interview performance, and in everything they do and say about their next job.

There are plenty of guides to the ideal CV, but pick any model and you will get criticism from the marketplace. Career changers receive all kinds of conflicting advice about CVs, not realising that recruitment specialists and employers often have very different requirements. Is there a right kind of CV? Only in one sense – a CV that gets *you* through the door into an interview. While it would be tempting to offer a single, one-size-fits-all solution, it won't wash. There are a range of models in this book and two formats that I would give a great deal of attention to if I were looking for a new job tomorrow. Sadly, for the reader who likes life to be clear-cut, they pull in opposite directions – but, depending on what you want to achieve, *all* the recommended CV models in this book work.

Everyone wants a quick fix CV. Some people pay to have a CV written. Many type in "CV" into Google and take whatever advice they can find. Others rely on the (rather mixed) views of friends, HR specialists or recruiters. Take time to think through what you need and write a CV that works as a door-opener for you. Very few candidates write a good CV quickly – it takes time and reflection, and some market testing. Fewer still understand that just writing a CV is not enough – it needs to be an integrated part of a broader message.

This book is written in three sections. If you want to start writing a CV today, skip to Part 2. If you want to think about why you are writing it and how it will be read, consult Part 1. If you want to know how to make the best use of a well-crafted CV in shaping your next career move, explore Part 3. Happy hunting.

☑ **Part 1**
Understanding CVs
and Their Impact

☐ **Part 2**
Composing Your
CV

☐ **Part 3**
Making Your CV
Work For You

Getting Your Message Across

This chapter helps you to:

I Understand the power and impact of well-pitched CVs, covering letters, emails and other key documents in the job-search process

I Know how and why a CV is used in today's labour market

I See your CV and other documents as part of a coherent message

I Start building your personal brand

"You don't write because you want to say something, you write because you have something to say."

F Scott Fitzgerald

YOUR LIFE ON PAPER

A CV is a document that sits uncomfortably between old and new ways of doing things. The title "Curriculum Vitae" (which some hopefuls mistakenly include as a title) gives it away. A *curriculum vitae* didn't just summarise your life, but indicated that you were the kind of person with a classical education or at least a passing understanding of Latin. To have a curriculum vitae (and to call it that) suggested that you were an educated professional. After all, before the 1960s most manual workers rarely needed to fill in application forms.

The US and Canadian equivalent "résumé" is not much less quaint, conveying that characteristic American love–hate relationship with the French language: it implies something classy but, pronounced without a hint of a French accent, it becomes a term that seems classless and accessible by all (the word résumé, "summary", is never used by the French for this document – they say "CV").

An interesting clue about the perceived tone of "curriculum vitae" is that it is still used in medical and academic circles in North America. In American English, a "CV" is a longer document than a résumé, and includes a more comprehensive professional history including details of every role, publications and special contributions or significant achievements. In certain professions, it may even include samples of the person's work and may run to many pages. In contrast, in the USA a résumé is seen as a summary – typically no more than two pages – highlighting only key items of information.

In the UK, "curriculum vitae" has relaxed into the more user friendly "see-vee". The condensed "CV" conveys a sharp, focused business document, but its old-fashioned origins still linger. It comes from a time when a lot more was understated; things were simply understood by picking up all the right kind of cultural clues. Even today, having a "good" school, established university and a few blue-chip companies or top consultancies listed is a pretty good door-opener. A curriculum vitae just gave the right headlines. The unwritten rule was that you simply stated the facts – school, qualifications, job titles, broad areas of responsibility. The recruiter did the rest – making all kinds of assumptions about ability based largely on social background and exposure to the right organisations.

That worked in the days of a curriculum vitae. There were, at that time, far fewer occupational pathways and a much smaller range of qualifications. And, in any event, only the professional classes needed or used a CV – and then only rarely. A great deal of recruitment was done using application forms, which required even less creativity, or was based on word-of-mouth introductions and an interview of varying quality and inventiveness, let alone relationship to the job.

The world of jobs and recruitment has changed radically since then. There are now thousands of careers open to people from thousands of backgrounds. Even more significantly, as far as this book is concerned, a "CV" is no longer read the same way. The sheer volume of applications and the information overload we all experience means that it is read quickly, sometimes by someone with only a passing understanding of the role in question. It is often read in search of keywords, key phrases, skills expressed in a specific terms.

A CV is read with far less attention to personality than it would have been 25 years ago ("quirky" now looks more like "unlikely fit"). It is read with far less tolerance for potential, and far more focus on what you have actually done. It is read by someone hunting for quick, well-presented evidence that you can do the job.

HOW CVS ARE USED IN OTHER CULTURES

CVs have different formats in different cultures. For example:

- In German-speaking countries a photograph is often mandatory. In Britain and the US this would be perceived as potentially discriminatory, as the age, sex and race of the applicant are immediately visible in a photograph.

- In some European countries it is still useful to indicate whether you have fulfilled any obligation to undertake military service.

- In Germany you need to send a covering letter with your "*Lebenslauf*" (CV), and also include a passport photograph, school certificates and other qualifications, plus testimonials of previous employment.

- In Japan you require a "*Rirekisho*", more of a personal profile than a showcase for your talents. Japanese employers place great emphasis on potential for training, and how workers fit into the team. The document should be handwritten in Japanese.

- In the USA and sometimes in the UK you see a "target statement" or "objective statement" at the top of the document (such as "Looking for an entry-level position in _____"). This was strongly encouraged in the US during the mid-1990s but has since fallen out of favour.

- In the USA candidates do not include their date of birth, marital status or details of their family. This information is also rapidly disappearing from British CVs – since the introduction of age discrimination legislation in 2006 candidates are no longer expected to include their age or date of birth.

- In France and Japan candidates are normally expected to provide handwritten covering letters that are subject to scrutiny by graphologists, who believe that handwriting gives away aspects of personality. In the UK graphology is considered to be no more reliable than astrology as a predictor of workplace performance.

TRENDS AND FADS

CVs have always been subject to fads and preferences. Here are some of the most recent trends:

- Most employers outside the academic world now prefer a reverse chronological CV (your most recent job comes first).

- Recruiters and employers vary widely in their views on the use of a "profile" (a short paragraph setting out your skills and experiences or summarising your career to date and your potential). Many candidates now open their CV with such a statement, but some decision makers still do not like a profile of any kind.

- Listing IT skills was a strong differentiator during the 1980s, but these skills are now such common currency that they are often not mentioned in management CVs.

- There have been debates between the "chronological" CV (job by job, usually starting with the most recent) and the "functional" CV (structured as a list of key skills and competencies taken from various parts of a candidate's work history). The functional format is sometimes used by those who have little work experience or by those who want to make a change in their career.

- From the late 1990s onwards in the UK there has been greater acceptance by recruiters of a stand-alone list of key achievements and experiences (although some recruiters prefer to extract this from a job-by-job history).

- The jury is out about hobbies and background interests. Some employers say they never look at this information or it is irrelevant, others say that it gives a more rounded picture.

- In the past when CVs were retyped only rarely they would often include the names of long-term referees. This is now considered inadvisable, at least in the UK market – you have no idea how and when a CV will be circulated, and it is best to brief a referee about each specific position.

- The last decade has also seen the impact of CVs loaded onto Internet Job Boards or employer websites, and also a high proportion of CVs are now sent electronically by email rather than by post.

The biggest change in recent times is that we compose and type CVs ourselves. In the pre-computer world a senior manager would never touch a keyboard, and so would ask a relative or a secretary to type up a CV, often as a quiet favour to begin a discreet job hunt. In fact, this has led to a CV revolution. Five or 10 years ago, even in an age of word processing, job seekers changed little on their CV whenever they wanted to go back to the job market. They probably added details regarding their most recent job and training, made sure it all fitted and printed it off. We now live in an age of personalisation – personal weblogs, MP3 players churning out personal playlists … . Now more and more technologically savvy career changers are producing highly focused, targeted CVs.

WHAT IS A CV FOR?

Most job seekers believe that their CV needs to say everything important about themselves that might help get them a job. They are entirely wrong. A CV isn't there to get you a job. It's there to get you into a meeting. This might be an interview (with an employer or with a recruitment consultant), it might be a networking meeting, it might be the opportunity to pitch for a piece of work. In other words, a CV is a piece of communication that has only one purpose: to get you into a room with someone who can influence your future.

Once you realise that, it changes the way you think about your **message**. And it's important to realise that your CV is not your message – it is part of it. Your message is everything you communicate about yourself on paper, by email or in a conversation. Your message is like a branding message for a product: it needs to be coherent, memorable and effective. Writing an effective CV, therefore, is not enough. You need to think about everything that you say about yourself. Some people have strong CVs but fail to take the same approach when they fill in an application form. Others are strong at interview, but fail to write a document that gets them the interview in the first place.

One of the reasons you might find this book useful is the biggest problem of all: many jobseekers have a CV that fails to get them shortlisted – not because of a lack of skills or experience, simply because it doesn't work. Chapter 3 covers the main reasons why CVs underperform or miss their target, but one point stands out: in a competitive marketplace you need the best CV you are capable of writing.

It's sadly true that in a job interview it is rarely the best candidate who gets the job. It's the person who puts in the best interview performance. Similarly, the best candidate doesn't necessarily get shortlisted for interview – it's the person with the most appropriate and effective CV.

FOCUSING ON YOUR PERSONAL BRAND

Chapter 2 will go into a lot more detail about the opinions and preferences employers hold about your CV. Before looking at the way a good CV is composed, it's important to think of it as a coherent message that expresses an important brand – *you*.

Businesses spend millions every year creating, building and supporting brand messages. A car manufacturer launching a new car in 2 years' time naturally puts a huge effort into the car's design and engineering, but puts equal focus on the new model as a brand in its own right. The name matters – often established carefully through focus groups from different markets and different countries. Then comes the image – who is the car aimed at? What kind of reactions will prospective customers come up with? A multi-million dollar campaign follows, all aimed to do one thing – to influence everything that likely buyers will think, say and do when that brand name is mentioned.

A good CV is part of your brand identity. This may sound like an out-landish suggestion – what you're doing is, of course, far more modest than an international marketing campaign. But even though the scale is different, the principles hold true.

Brand Identity

How a brand is built up	Product and service marketing	Your personal brand
Planning	Looking carefully at what the market needs or might need in the future	Focusing in a disciplined way on what employers actually need
Design	How will the product/service work? How will it offer actual or perceived benefits to the customer?	How far does your work history and skill set convey that you will add value?
Awareness	How can you make likely customers aware that your service exists? How will they think or feel about it when they first hear about it?	How can you make potential hirers aware that you exist? How will they think or feel about you when they first hear about you?
Anticipated impact	What is the first impression of a potential customer when coming across the product/service? What impact will it have when used?	What is the first impression of an employer looking at your CV and covering letter? How will you add to this at interview?
		continued

Competition	What products/services are already out there, what do they have to offer, and how can you add value, variation or difference?	What is the typical profile of someone hired to do the job you want? What is the profile of a top 10% performer? How can you stand out from the crowd, especially if your background is not conventional?
Experience	How far are a customer's initial expectations met or challenged when using the product or service?	How far does your interview (and job) perform-ance match the claims made in your CV?
Reputation	How can you build on your brand through word-of-mouth referral?	How can you use networking to improve your job search through word-of-mouth referral?
Forward planning	Once a brand is established and effective, what spin-off products and services can you develop, building on the original brand name and values?	Once in a job, how can you continue to ensure that others in the marketplace remain aware that you are updating your skills?

Making personal branding work

The important thing about a brand, whether it is a brand owned by a multi-national company or your own personal branding, is that it must be coherent, communicable and memorable.

Being **communicable** and **memorable** means that it needs to be some-thing that explains itself when you are not there. That's the definition of good job application documents – your CV and your covering let-ter or a well-completed application form. Too many candidates say "when I explain that part of my CV I have no problems". That's a bit like saying "once you take the product home you'll see its benefits". Your CV is a document designed to be read (initially, anyway) in your absence, without your footnotes, explanations or code-breaking.

Secondly, being communicable means saying something that the reader can understand, and saying it quickly. This is about being **coherent**. Weak CVs contain many overlapping messages. The confused recruiter starts juggling conflicting ideas ("looks like a frustrated accountant, maybe into people development, but also looks like he wants to work in the health sector – I'm confused"). The CV looks interesting, but goes on the "maybe" pile. Up against dozens if not hundreds of hopefuls, "maybe" is pretty close to "not suitable".

Being coherent also means that different parts of your offering have to match up. The style, content and "feel" of your covering letter and CV or other documents should match, and should all communicate the same themes. More importantly, your interview content and performance should be a close match to your documents. Recruiters commonly complain that a very different person walks in the door to the one they were expecting – which can be positive as well as negative. Make sure that your CV sells you well on paper – that means selling the real you, not one that looks like your idea of an identikit candidate.

TRUE OR FALSE? – EMPLOYER CYNICISM ABOUT CVs

There are few recruiters out there who believe everything you put on paper. Occupational psychologists have for many years written about "impression management" – the way candidates attempt to manipulate the perception of the recruiter. Some HR specialists use the phrase as if it means "lying". It doesn't – all interpersonal situations at work where we are trying to influence someone involve some kind of impression management: in a sales meeting you want to appear knowledgeable and trustworthy, in a negotiation you want to appear confident, in a meeting with your boss you may want to appear focused, creative, decisive, and so on.

It's perfectly acceptable to think about the way your overall message works to shape the way people see you. That's how personal branding operates. The important thing is to reveal *the best version of yourself*, not to try to pass yourself off as someone else. Do bear in mind, however, that recruiters are highly tuned to information that seems overblown, improbable or just plain false.

A research study published by the international HR consultancy Cubiks in July 2006 revealed that many employers doubt the accuracy of claims made by candidates. The study revealed that "lies and exaggerations have become common features of application forms and CVs". Only 12% of employers believed they never see fictitious information. Fifty-nine per cent of survey respondents stated that they have had to withdraw job offers at the very last minute following the receipt of a poor personal reference undermining the claims made by a candidate.

Our own survey (see Chapter 2) reinforces the suspicion in the minds of decision makers. The other side of the coin is that if you're writing a CV you are under considerable pressure to provide accurate and reliable information. As one recruiter put it "better the reliable, dull candidate than the exciting dud".

So, be aware that your CV will be read by someone busy, unsympathetic to your long-term career needs and, possibly, someone who starts with the assumption that you will not be telling the truth. Secondly, be aware that writing a good CV is only part of the process of getting your message right.

How Employers React to CVs

This chapter helps you to:

▪ Understand how employers interpret CVs

▪ Spot employer likes and dislikes

▪ Understand recent trends in CV writing

▪ Know what makes a CV effective

▪ Understand what might make your CV irritating

Words are, of course, the most powerful drug used by mankind.
Rudyard Kipling

UNDERSTANDING THE WAY YOUR CV WILL BE READ

How do you decide what your CV should look like, and what it should contain? Many people, particularly recruiters, have strong opinions about what they like to see in a CV. You might, however, think that the most important view comes from employers themselves, particularly human resources specialists, as they decide who is called for interview, and who gets the job.

As it is vital to find out exactly what HR staff are thinking, a special research survey was commissioned for this book. The research was conducted by Career Management Consultants Ltd (CMC), one of the UK's top outplacement companies. CMC's specialism is outplacement (career coaching for executives and senior managers, paid for by the organisations who are making them redundant). CMC has therefore provided one-to-one career coaching to thousands of senior managers and executives over the years, and as a result spends a lot of time working closely with HR specialists.

The survey, undertaken in 2007, went out to over 7300 HR directors and managers, making it one of the most extensive CV surveys undertaken in recent years. A wide range of responses were received, many of them expressing specific likes and dislikes, and defining best and worst practice.

HR vs recruiter perspective

While reading the survey results, be aware that this is only one perspective. The respondents in our survey were HR directors and managers, and also line managers with hiring responsibility in organisations. They are vitally important people in the recruitment process, because they make the final selection decision.

Do remember, however, that there is another group of important people out there – recruiters. They have different titles, depending on the level of staff they place. At the lower end of the market you can find employment or staffing agencies, many of whom will deal largely with temporary or contract work. Agencies working at higher levels tend to call themselves recruitment or selection consultancies, while those operating at the most senior end usually title themselves executive search and selection consultancies (the "search" part of their activity means they actively hunt down suitable candidates, which is why they are also called "headhunters"). As various chapters of this book point out, recruiters have different preferences about CVs.

CV TRENDS

This survey provides insights into the way a large number of employers in today's marketplace think about the CV as a recruitment tool. Employers make the following comments about trends they have spotted in the last 2 years:

- "The electronic age means that often no real thought goes into submitting an application – you can just bang it out to a number of companies via email."

- "Poor standards of grammar and spelling."

- "Too much, rather than too little data."

- "CVs are generally better presented and tailored to job they are applying for. Agency CVs have been getting worse – just cutting and pasting without any thought as to presentation."

- "Increased number of unsolicited CVs via email."

- "Applications from younger applicants are shoddy. They don't seem to get the right direction at school regarding how to do this – or perhaps they don't listen. Many younger applicants just don't make enough effort – even university graduates."

Strong points

HR specialists point to a number of areas where CVs are particularly effective or memorable, including:

- "Shorter, more focused CVs."

- "More information provided about skills – particularly transferable skills."

- "There now seems to be an almost standardised template used, which makes a recruiter's job much easier."

- "Increased use of profiles or key skills as one of the first items on the CV."

- "Good covering letters being succinct and addressing the relevant issues."

- "Applicants' IT skills are increasing and as a result some CVs received are almost a work of art. They have considered the role they have applied for and adapted their CV accordingly. It shows more of a thought process when applying for roles."

What employers find immediately off-putting

Two respondents cut to the heart of the problem: "Most CVs do not answer the question of why an interview should be offered for that role" ... "the number of applicants, who on the basis of their CV, have no idea about whether or not they have the right credentials for the job applied for". Here are some of the things that employers tell you will pretty much guarantee that your CV hovers over the waste-paper bin:

- "CVs on coloured paper, using lots of different fonts."

- "Over-the-top selling of candidates' abilities in CV jargon."

- "People just sending in a CV with no covering letter indicating which post they are applying for."

- "Cutting and pasting from other applications without changing the company's name!"

- "Over-egging skills and achievements."

- "CVs that look as if they came out of a book, e.g. *I'm a team player but I can work alone.*"

- "The use of buzz words and jargon."

- "Profiles which are just standard wording."

- "Too much irrelevant personal information, e.g. names of children."

- "CVs with acronyms, particularly technical terms, where initials can have several meanings."

- "Copies of certificates, including Scouts knot badge."

- "Dump of detailed job description for every job held."

- "CVs put together years ago and updated in pen."

HOW SHOULD I SEND IN MY CV?

This is how employers would prefer your CV to arrive:

By email	49%
By email and by post	15%
By post	12%
No preference	24%.

Some would argue that your best strategy might be to send by email *and* by post. Be as careful with an email covering letter as you would be with one sent on paper. Views on this topic included the following:

- "When emailing covering letters, people can use poor grammar and be too informal, which they would never do in a letter sent in the post."

- "Email is great but does allow people to be more sloppy when submitting information."

- "Internet recruitment often leads to candidates submitting their CVs for vacancies regardless of whether or not they really want the job. No care is taken and the CVs often bear no relation to the job on offer."

- "Emailing CVs has made things quicker – it's easier for HR to get the CV to the line manager quickly in this format. It means you can make decisions quicker."

One smaller employer complained when CVs are sent in only by email because then someone has the job of printing them off.

Binding your CV, putting it in a cover and other special effects

Only one employer in every 100 wants to see your CV in a binder or cover. One dispirited writer complained of "the use of wacky fonts with the idea of making the CV stand out. People think it makes them come across as a fun person where as I feel it shows a lack of professionalism."

Including a photograph

Only 2% of employers would strongly agree with the proposition that a photograph should be included, while nearly 90% are either indifferent or opposed to the idea. A photograph creates legal problems for employers as a photograph immediately communicates gender, race and age.

Reports indicated that some candidates sent in photographs described as off-putting or distracting. Some candidates sent in photographs as big as A4. Many respondents went out of their way to list the use of a photograph as one of their main hates.

Who will read my CV?

It's interesting to find out exactly who reads your CV first. In answer to the question "Who performs the first sift of CVs in your organisation?" the survey revealed that most CVs sent to organisations are read by qualified HR staff (55%) or by line managers (29%).

The message seems to be that if you know your CV is more likely to be read by a line manager, write it with that person in mind. However, in most cases it needs to be written so that it will appeal to both a qualified HR person or a line manager.

THE STRUCTURE OF YOUR CV

How many pages?

Two-thirds of employers would prefer your CV to be no more than two pages long. Only 20% feel that a CV of three pages is acceptable, 8% have no preference and a small minority – 3% of HR specialists – would like to see a CV expressed in just one page. A large proportion of HR managers said that CVs have become shorter and more focused, although a few expressed exactly the opposite view – one indicated that he had received a 45-page CV.

Summary information on page 1

Many CVs begin with a profile; a short paragraph summarising your history and your strengths. This book will explore the pros and cons of such an approach.

Some employers say they dislike profiles on the first page of CVs. One wrote that "personal summaries are irritating – they take up valuable space and no one is ever going to say they are not a team player or enthusiastic or capable! I never give them any credence". Another view was that "profiles at the start of many CVs read like the foreword of a Superman novel". Another complained that profiles were often just a repeat of historical information contained elsewhere in the CV.

More than 80% of HR specialists do prefer to see a short profile or summary on the first page of the CV. One respondent felt that the CV profile "appears to have become more realistic and less a statement of what the individual thinks he/she should say". Seventy-seven per cent of employers say they would like a list of key achievements on the first page, and only 7% said they did not find this information useful.

The question of whether or not you should use a profile and a summary of your skills, experience and achievements is an open one – see Part 2 of this book to help you decide what will work for you.

What order should I list my jobs in?

Responses suggest that most employers (73%) prefer to see your jobs listed with the most recent job detailed first. Only 18% prefer to see a CV with your most recent job last.

Reasons for each job change

Sixty-one per cent of employers are actively interested in knowing the reasons for job change. See Chapter 10 before including this information.

Most recent salary

Seventy per cent of HR specialists express a preference for candidates to include details of your most recent salary. Again, see Chapter 10 on this controversial topic.

Things you do outside work

It's worth listing details of voluntary activities. Ninety per cent of employers are either happy to see information of this kind or have no strong feelings either way. Slightly fewer, 84%, are prepared to look at details of your hobbies. One respondent took a positive view: "I want to know a bit about them as a person: travel, pastimes, as well as qualifications and experience". Others complained about too much irrelevant, personal information.

Listing your competencies

As Chapter 12 of this book discusses, a number of employers are asking candidates for information about competencies (a competency is a developed summary of a skill, which also takes account of underpinning knowledge, attitude, skill level and motivation). Some CVs offer a list of half a dozen or so competencies on page 1 in order to provide this information immediately. Fourteen per cent of employers have no interest in seeing your competencies listed, but 56% find this a useful addition to a CV, and about a third of employers have no preference in this matter.

A CV that has obviously been written by a professional CV writing service or by an agency

A number of people in our survey expressed some frustration with professionally written CVs. One manager found them "too polished". A very significant 71% of employers disagreed with the suggestion that a professionally written CV is useful. Many employers clearly include in this bracket CVs written by recruitment consultancies. One respondent complained that "more people are using professional agencies, which takes away any personalisation of your CV". Another wrote "Many CVs from people sharing the same professional CV advice will look the same and use identical 'search-enhancing' words and phrases." Another complained of "the degree of sameness due to coaching". A further complaint was that CVs written by a third party tend to be "too short on information".

Be careful if an agency wants to rewrite your CV: "It is not unusual to receive a professionally produced, word-perfect CV, which has clearly not been produced by the candidate, accompanied by an email containing several very basic spelling errors". Ask to see a copy before it is sent anywhere. One HR manager wrote that "Employment agencies who edit CVs on behalf of candidates often alter the documents so they misrepresent applicants". Many employers dislike agency-submitted CVs because they "refer to the candidate as a number".

CV CONTENT

CVs with no email address

The failure to include an email address is a major reason for exclusion. A massive 93% of employers indicate that this is something they would prefer to see in a CV.

References

A great many CVs include the names and addresses of referees. Our research indicates that this is preferred by less than a third of employers. About 70% either don't mind or would rather you didn't waste space including this information, so the clear view, for reasons explained later in this book, is that references shouldn't be included in a CV.

Your qualifications

Far too many CVs begin with information about school qualifications. Roughly a third of employers would prefer to see details of A Level or GCSE grades, a third are indifferent and a third would rather not be sent this information. There is no suggestion that employers are any more interested in A Level grades than in GCSE grades.

The topic of how you deal with your qualifications is deal with in considerable depth in other chapters in this book.

Languages

If you have strong spoken languages, list them. Eighty-one per cent of employers are interested in reading about them.

Willingness to relocate

A surprising 70% of employers actively want to know from a CV whether you are prepared to relocate for a new job.

Age-related information

One of the reasons for asking employers about CVs in 2007 was to see the impact of recent age discrimination legislation. The evidence suggests that most job seekers are confused about what they should or should not include. Some candidates believe that they should not include any dates in their CVs at all. The evidence suggests that these CVs would not be acceptable to most employers.

Whilst acknowledging the need to comply with the law, the following percentage of HR professionals state that the following details are useful in a CV:

Start and end dates for different roles	97%
Details of jobs held more than 10 years ago	46%
Date a degree or professional qualification was obtained	60%.

One HR manager wrote: "Some employment agencies have presented CVs without any dates of previous employment as they have misunderstood the age discrimination legislation. The dates are required to ascertain the applicants employment history, e.g. how long they stay in a position, not to work out how old they are".

Another took this view: "The removal of dates makes it much harder to trace a candidate's career path and check any gaps (which our referencing company would do anyway once an offer has been made)".

Telling the truth

For at least the last 20 years, the rule of thumb amongst recruiters was that one CV in 10 takes liberties with the truth. According to the CMC survey, most employers feel that candidates lie about something in their CV. Employers were asked, based on the CVs they have seen, what proportion contain false information. Two facts came through:

- Nearly half of employers believe that at one in 10 candidates lie about qualifications.

- Seventy-four per cent of employers believe that candidates give untrue information about job titles.

- Fifty-one per cent have experience of candidates giving false information about their training.

- Employers also find that candidates provide untrue information about the reasons for leaving previous jobs, accountability within positions, dates, achievements and hobbies.

Covering letters

"Poor quality or overly obsequious covering letters" were criticised by one HR team. Others complained of unfocused letters, many containing poor grammar or spelling. The recommendation from one recruiter is that candidates "should still include a covering letter – even if they are emailing a CV. Lots of people have stopped doing this, losing the opportunity to give a flavour of why you are interested in a particular company".

Pet hates

Answers vary, but you can see some common trends from the following list:

- "Fancy folders, gimmicks (e.g. attaching a teabag and a message which says 'have a cup of tea while you read this'). I even heard of someone sending half a £50 note saying the other half would be handed over at interview!"

- "What irritates me is someone applying for a role when they have no relevant skills, qualifications or experience."

- "People applying for a role when they are not available for 6 months to a year."

- "Overselling commitment and enthusiasm."

- "Lack of ability to spell-check."

- "Language used that is more suitable to a dating agency!"

Quality of CVs

One unexpected outcome of our survey was the fact that a number of respondents volunteered the information that CVs have improved in recent years. One wrote: "CVs are generally better thoughout now and there are few really poor ones". Other comments about improving quality included:

- "More people are now taking their time when putting together CVs meaning that the information is much more succinct and easier to read."

- "Reduction in number of pages – better clarity around role tasks/ skills/abilities."

- "Many candidates learning to put themselves 'up front' rather than their academic history."

- "Contain less self-praise and more objectivity around responsibilities and achievements."

- "Brevity is a continually pleasing trend."

- "Seem to be becoming more 'user friendly' with the most important data on the first page."

IMPLICATIONS OF THE SURVEY

All very interesting, you might think, but how does this help? Remember that these views represent the perspective of HR specialists and line managers. As this book will explain, external recruiters see your CV in a very different light.

However, this survey does help focus on the fact that employers do have distinct preferences about what they want to see in a CV, and where. There is evidence to suggest that employers strongly favour CVs that contain clear information relevant to the job. The evidence also suggests that employers are positively influenced by well-structured CVs free of inaccuracies, which contain correct and focused information.

Secondly, employers do want to know key information from your past, including dates of employment and qualifications. This is worth bearing in mind if you are trying to make sense of age discrimination law. Finally, be aware of what immediately impresses or puts off an employer – it could make the difference between the "yes" or the "no" pile on the first sift. CMC's CV survey therefore provides a very useful starting point for writing a CV that achieves its purpose.

CV Basics

This chapter helps you to:

I Learn from other people's mistakes

I Spot the things that irritate recruiters

I Avoid traps, clangers and generally shooting yourself in the foot

I Work out what goes in your CV, and what stays out

"What is written without effort is in general read without pleasure."
Samuel Johnson

WHERE AND WHY CVs FAIL TO DELIVER
Your 15 seconds of fame

According to Andy Warhol, everyone lives in the hope of achieving just 15 minutes of fame. Every time you present your CV you have an even tighter goal – 15 seconds of someone's attention. While writing a CV few of us think about how little time a recruiter will spend reading it.

Estimates of the average attention given to a CV vary – anything between 15 and 30 seconds. This is half true. It is true in the sense that any recruiter who has to deal with over 100 CVs is going to have to find a way of sifting through them very fast – scanning them (usually by eye) for key phrases or pieces of information to make an interview shortlist. You may think that an interview is just a conversation, but it's expensive to arrange and even more expensive to put one or more professional staff into a room all day. So organisations need to pre-select just the ones that look most suited to the job. A first sift (also known as "pre-selection" or "top slicing") is usually required to cut the pile down. On this first sift a busy recruiter will be speed-reading your CV or parts of it. In our CV survey one busy HR manager wrote: "Summarise what your employer does and who they do it for. Tell me what it is that I need to know in as concise and as easily readable format as you possibly can in order that I can make sense of your CV. If I am scanning around 500 CVs for a role, my first-pass filter of them is measured in seconds rather than minutes".

Career coach Kate Howlett of Ruspini Consulting reminds us that: "only 7% of the population actually read anything. The rest of us scan-read. Our eye line follows certain areas of the page which means that we should put the most important facts in our CV in the key areas of the page and go with the natural eye flow". These methods are consciously used in advertising and explains why certain parts of a newspaper page are more expensive to advertise in than others. Eye flow theory suggests that readers fix very briefly on key points in the text – often the areas that are highlighted in some way or in bold print.

On message, on time

So how much time will a recruiter spend reading your CV? It is unlikely to be more than 5 minutes even in the most painstaking of organisations. If it's a skim-read, it may be as little as 15–20 seconds. What other kinds of documents do you spend 15 seconds reading? You will give more attention to the cornflakes packet. Fifteen seconds is about the time you would spend reading an advertisement in a newspaper or magazine, or a poster in an underground station. And yet, most CVs are written as if they were the kind of document you would read in depth – a business report, a short story or an instruction manual. Any document should be written with only one principle in mind: what the reader needs to see.

In the past shortlisting was often performed on grounds that have little to do with the job – sex, age, personal background. This can still happen (for example, it's fairly easy to guess at a candidate's age, particularly if they include details of their job history and qualifications), but it's not the only unfair method. A good, well-presented CV for an average candidate will always get through a first sift with greater certainty than an unfocused CV for an above-average candidate.

At some stage you'll have asked yourself why you didn't get invited to an interview for a job you feel you could do in your sleep. Why didn't your CV work? The problem faced by many candidates is that they really can't answer the question. Worse still, they have a sense that perhaps only half the CV works, but they are not sure which half.

Out and out blunders

In our CV research we asked HR specialists to give us examples of the typos, howlers and unintended comedy that creeps into CVs. Here's a selection of their answers: the following were typed into actual CVs:

- "I always apply myself 10% to everything I do."

- "I pay meticuououls attention to detail."

- "I worked as shelf stacker in a supper market."

- "Hobbies: I enjoy eating pizzas."

- "In all my previous roles I have been inellectually challenged."

- "As duty manager with XXXX Hotels I have a wealth of experience of customer complaints."

- "Job was too busy so I left because of metal fatigue."

- "I was unable to respond to the demands of the Credit Controller. I left the country and unfortunately returned an older and wizened person. I could go on but I intend to write my own book."

- "Wholly responsible for two failed financial institutions."

Do watch out for unintentional humour that bites back at you. One employer reported: "Just received a CV today which included a photo. The individual was overweight and talked in his first paragraph about significant 'expansion experience'".

Being "creative"

One thing is crystal clear from our survey in Chapter 2. Avoid a CV that uses special effects to grab attention by using coloured ink or paper, laminated sheets, a photograph or presentation in a smart folder. But other kinds of special effects will be equally unacceptable: fancy fonts, tables, boxes or columns, graphics or cartoons. Something, perhaps, which looks like this:

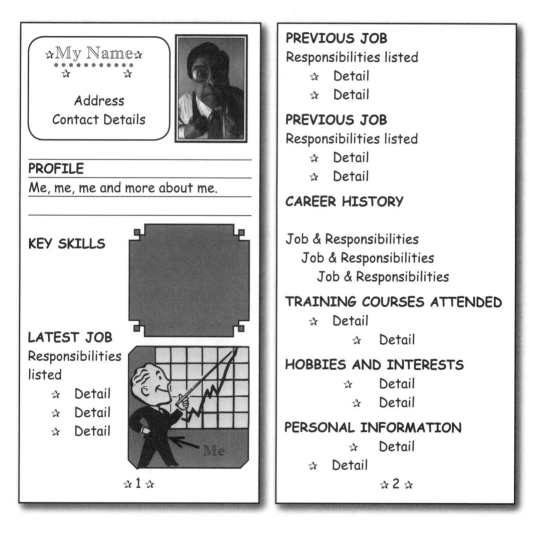

At face value, you might think that something that has high visual impact would work without fail. Compared to the average simple black and white, text-only CV, surely it will stand out? Yes. For all the wrong reasons. It draws attention to its quirkiness, not the information it contains. It contains features that are universally disliked by decision makers. A photograph may mean that it is inadmissible in an equal opportunities selection process.

Generally employers will only look at your CV if it is word processed or typed and presented on clean, white paper. Only 1% of employers in our survey wants your CV to arrive in a binder. One HR manager, however, proved that there is an exception to every rule: "I was most impressed by a candidate who at the time clearly did not have access to a PC and submitted a beautifully handwritten detailed CV. He had clearly taken the time and effort to do this for each position he was applying for – the CV submitted was an original, not copied, and tailored to the requirements of the job. Needless to say, he got an interview on the strength of this".

Presentation

While content matters more than anything, the overall look of your CV is important too.

Do:

✓ Allow plenty of white space around the text.

✓ Use a clear, modern font such as Arial.

✓ Print your CV on good-quality (100 gsm) white paper – nothing fancier.

✓ Make sure that paragraphs and bullet points are aligned.

✓ Write in short, focused sentences and paragraphs. Think newspaper article style rather than business report.

✓ Make sure that the most important points in your CV stand out clearly, just as you would expect key messages to stand out in any form of published advertisement.

✓ Post your CV unfolded to preserve its visual impact.

Don't:

✗ Try to squeeze too much information onto one page – edit instead.

✗ Send out a poor-quality photocopy of a CV.

✗ Include a photograph.

✗ Mix fonts or sizes (with the exception that you can put your name across the top in a slightly larger font).

✗ Bind your CV in a folder, laminate it or do anything with it other than staple the pages together in the top left-hand corner.

✗ Fax your CV except in an emergency – it ends up looking like a very poor-quality document.

Words, words …

CVs aren't difficult once you've got the words right.

Do:

✓ Communicate in the simplest language you can. Short words work.

✓ Make sure that your CV includes all of the relevant keywords or phrases that would be flagged up if your CV text is being searched electronically.

Don't:

✗ Overuse the word "I" – it can sound like either a begging letter or an ego trip (see Chapter 8 for ways of writing that avoid this).

✗ Put "Curriculum Vitae" at the top.

✗ Repeat text in your CV. If you've said it, you've said it.

✗ Use obscure abbreviations, acronyms or jargon.

✗ Misspell, as many candidates do, your job title or the name of your current employer.

✗ Allow typos, grammatical errors or spelling mistakes to get through into the final version of your CV. If in doubt, don't be proud – get it checked by a perfectionist who swallowed a dictionary at an early age.

First draft

It really is best not to start by adapting your old CV. Few of us have the toughness to really edit our own material. It's far better to have forgotten what went in your earlier CVs and start afresh.

Do:

✓ Write your first draft CV in relation to a particular, real job. You will find that this helps you to be focused rather than cataloguing everything.

✓ Try doing some separate listing of your skills and achievements before you begin writing your CV.

✓ Make sure your work history is presented in the right order and check, check, check that the dates match up.

✓ Try to offer short, uncomplicated explanations for any gaps in your CV.

✓ If it helps, write a long (four- or five-page) version first, and then cut it right back.

✓ Begin by using the suggested structures in this book. You can always adapt this basic model afterwards.

✓ Start by writing page 2 first.

Don't:

✗ Kid yourself that you can get away with dusting off your old CV, unless you have evidence that it works without question.

✗ Rush the job. It takes a good 4 hours or so to put together a good, polished CV, and you can't do that in a single 4-hour block. Draft, redraft, get feedback, draft again, check for a market reaction, finalise.

Designing text layout for maximum impact

Advertising specialists tell us that readers scan a page of text very quickly, their eyes following a z-shaped path down the page. This means that text that forms clear lines across the page commands attention, and also means that any keywords you use should appear on the left-hand side of the page.

Do:

✓ Put the strongest statement at the beginning of each paragraph, and the strongest bullet point at the top of a list. Going for the dramatic finale works in the theatre but not here – there is no guarantee that the reader's eye will go deeper than the first sentence of each block of text.

✓ Put keywords close to the left-hand side of the paper or the beginning of a sentence.

✓ Use clear section headings without large gaps after them.

✓ Use bold text and, occasionally, capitals to attract the reader's eye.

Don't:

✗ Use a font size that looks small and cramped.

✗ Waste the very valuable left-hand side of the CV with information (e.g. dates) that doesn't make an impact.

✗ Right-justify your CV (aligned text on the right-hand margin) – it makes it difficult to read quickly.

✗ Overuse any text effects, such as text in bold or capitals.

✗ Use italics.

Tone

As most CVs look the same, oddities of tone tend to stand out. This can be effective as a way of getting remembered. More often it strikes entirely the wrong tone. You may be the kind of person who tends to put yourself down, but remember that it looks very different on paper – writing something like "my approach is a bit off the wall" or "I'm not as zany as people think!" will probably set off alarm bells, although you will probably still get away with "I enjoy thinking out of the box", even though it's a cliché.

Even more common is the tendency to apologise for things in the CV itself. Introducing a list of jobs as a "miscellany" or "unusual mix" is enough to convince the reader that you have no idea where your career is heading.

Do:

✓ Find a style and tone that matches your seniority.

✓ Use the same, businesslike, tone throughout.

✓ Above all else, give the reader of your CV what he or she wants to read.

Don't:

✗ Put yourself down.

✗ Try irony or humour. It rarely reads the way you want it to. Humour even in relation to interests often fails.

✗ Apologise for your CV or experience.

✗ Put anything that strikes a negative note, particularly on page 1.

✗ Draw attention to gaps and "problems".

✗ Include information just because you find it quaint or entertaining.

✗ Demonstrate frustration, envy, anger or a lust for revenge – save it for the punchbag in the gym.

Email

Not only does the lack of an email address condemn you to the "techno-dinosaur" bin, but interviews may only be arranged by email. Your only plan is to get connected – even if someone else sets it all up for you and you do nothing with your account except check your emails.

Do:

✓ Include an email address at the top of your CV.

✓ Use an email address that you check at least once a day.

Don't:

✗ Use a comical email address: "Happygolucky@freebie.com" sends entirely the wrong impression.

✗ Mistype your email address – if an employer gets a bounce-back they will be reluctant to try again.

Honesty

Whilst employers tell us (see Chapter 2) that a substantial percentage of CVs contain false information, lying in your CV is a quick route to disaster. As soon as something is discovered in an interview, your grave is dug. If you survive the interview and get the job, you may well face dismissal if you have presented false information. Dates, job titles and employment history can all be checked.

Be aware what information is already available about you. In the USA employers frequently use professional researchers to "Google" candidates, digging for background information (and sometimes discovering very public out-of-work activities that set off alarm bells).

It's easy to overdo "spin", but equally dangerous to let past events speak for themselves without interpretation. The reality is this. Your CV (and, later, your interview performance) should present you at your best. Nothing less. Recruiters sometimes accuse candidates and career coaches of "impression management" – but if you make no attempt to manage impressions, how do you hope to impress? The first question is always this – how far have you "spun" the facts away from the solid truth? If it's too far, what does that do to the integrity of your "offer"? But the bigger question is this – can you do the job?

Do:

✓ Present yourself in the best light possible light, in a credible way that sits within the parameters of checkable history.

✓ Stick to the facts as far as targets and figures are concerned.

Don't:

✗ Include information that you know is false.

✗ Deliberately include negative information, e.g. reasons for leaving your last job. You will, however, need to prepare an honest interview answer on this topic.

Your history

How far back should you go? In general, most employers only want to focus in detail on your last 5 years, and probably want only sketchy detail about jobs you did more than 10 years ago. The exception here, of course, is if you've been out of the workplace for the last few years. In this case you will need to refer to your most recent job, and you will probably have to write about jobs you did more than 10 years ago. For those returning to work after a gap, it is particularly important to choose a CV format that gives particular emphasis to your skills (see Chapter 5).

Do:

✓ Include details of voluntary work, community work, work placements and even temporary or contract jobs if they communicate skills.

✓ Give a short summary of the role and organisation every time you give details about a job.

Don't:

✗ Provide excessive detail about jobs you did more than 10 years ago.

✗ Include the full postal addresses of previous employers – town or city is sufficient for UK jobs.

✗ Use out-of-date terminology and jargon relating to older jobs – it dates you.

✗ Include months in the dates of beginning and ending jobs – keep it simple.

Skills

Skills, how you exercise them and your linked achievements, are the primary currency of your CV.

Do:

✓ Give plenty of detail about skills and achievements in your most recent two or three jobs.

✓ Use strong, one-word active verbs (e.g. *researched, organised, created, initiated, led, changed, transformed, built, shaped, influenced*) and avoid weak inactive verbs and phrases (*took part in, participated in, was responsible for, helped to manage…*).

✓ Write about concrete achievements (e.g. "Increased customer satisfaction rating from 80% to 96% in 12 months") rather than generalisations about activity ("Responsible for customer satisfaction").

Don't:

✗ Repeat details that are common to several jobs – use this information in the most recent job only.

✗ Begin a skill statement with "took part in …" or "we accomplished …". State what *you* did.

✗ Record skills or competencies that are also possessed by staff several rungs below you in the organisation.

✗ Mention failure unless you can talk about something useful you learned from the experience.

Qualifications

Employers indicate that they find information on qualifications useful. However, they are also aware that there are thousands of different courses and qualifications in the UK alone. Don't just list your qualifications – use information about them to support your message.

Do:

✓ List qualifications with grades if relevant and recent.

✓ Explain obscure initials or titles of qualifications – "translate" your qualifications into terms that are meaningful to an employer.

✓ Refer to study achievements when listing your skills, drawing out transferable skills (e.g. team working, investigation, planning).

✓ Explain qualifications that were obtained in another country – find out and state what their broad equivalent is in the UK.

Don't:

✗ List all your school-leaving qualifications (unless you left school very recently), particularly those you did up to the age of 16.

✗ Try to pretend you completed a qualification you didn't finish – state clearly how much of the course you attended, and what you got out of it.

✗ Include anything that looks incomplete or misleading, e.g. mentioning a degree without mentioning the subject or result.

✗ Show off your education or obscure knowledge by using phrases (e.g. Greek, Latin, scientific terms) that will confuse the average HR assistant (to say nothing of CV scanning software).

✗ Include details of qualifications that have been made out of date or irrelevant through other qualifications you have undertaken (if your last qualification was obtained over 15 years ago, minimal details may be sufficient).

Other information on your CV

Some people like to pack their CV with all kinds of quirky personal information including information about family, hobbies, pets, travel plans, being an Advanced Driver, religious affiliation, unfinished novels, pet prejudices and obsessions. Before you type in "Interests", stop. Is *any* of this relevant to a busy recruiter?

Do:

✓ Include some interests, just to make you appear a little more rounded.

✓ Include interests that demonstrate a degree of social contact, interaction or teamwork.

✓ Keep the personal information in your CV as brief as possible.

✓ State your availability and views on relocation in a covering letter if your home address is not close by to your target employer.

Don't:

✗ Put anything down under "Interests" unless (a) it has some relevance to the job or (b) you can talk inspiringly for at least 10 minutes on the subject.

✗ Talk for 10 minutes on the subject unless you are absolutely asked to do so.

✗ Waste space including details of your "full, clean driving licence" unless this is a stated job requirement.

✗ Include non-essential personal information e.g. height, weight, state of health, children/their names/ages, your religious or political beliefs.

✗ Refer to books, articles, academic works, etc., you have had published unless this information will be relevant to your employer.

✗ You will not normally need to provide copies of references or certificates with your CV – be prepared to produce relevant documents later in the process.

Age

The jury is still out about the impact of the age discrimination law introduced into the UK in 2006. This is particularly true in relation to the way you should write your CV. You should not normally make specific reference to your age. Some employers will require you not to give any dates at all – most of these will, however, require you to complete an application form.

Do:

✓ Include the start and end dates of jobs you have performed.

✓ Feel free to give only summary information about jobs you did more than 15 years ago or group them together (e.g. "From graduation to 1996 – Various engineering roles from Apprentice to Engineering Supervisor").

Don't:

✗ State your age or include your date of birth.

✗ Mention "GCE O Levels" on your CV – this automatically dates you as someone who probably left school before 1988.

✗ Mention your children's ages. Adult children give away your age, while mentioning the age of younger children opens up other problems – there never seems a good time for them to be moving schools. Only deal with this at interview, and then only if the issue is raised by the interviewer.

✗ List out-of-date qualifications unless you have to.

Reasons for each job change

Sixty-one per cent of employers in our survey say they are interested in knowing reasons for job change.

Do:

✓ Make sure your CV (for example in the profile) explains your reasons for changes in career direction.

✓ Prepare to be probed on this at interview.

Don't:

✕ Include specific reasons why you left a particular job, particularly factors that may suggest a negative relationship with a former employer as this information may get you rejected early in the process.

Most recent salary

Seventy per cent of HR specialists prefer candidates to include details of their most recent salary. Opinions among career coaches vary widely on this topic. Some recruiters insist that you should include a statement of your current or most recent salary. Their argument is that you are wasting an employer's time if you are being considered for a job paying far less than you are seeking. Other guides, including this one, suggest that this information may result in immediate exclusion, so is probably best left out of a CV (although, if requested, you may choose to provide this information in a covering letter).

Do:

✓ If requested, provide details of your most recent salary in a covering letter.

✓ Try to focus the conversation on what you are worth in the future, not what you are currently earning.

Don't:

✕ Include details of salary – present, past or hoped for – on the CV itself. Your CV should clearly represent your status and level of achievement. Everything else is a matter for negotiation.

See *Job Interviews: Top Answers To Tough Questions* for a range of tips on negotiating your starting salary.

Where Do You Want Your CV to Take You?

This chapter helps you to:

▌ Identify the kind of change you want to make

▌ Choose an appropriate CV format

▌ See the benefits of different CV styles

▌ Appreciate the variety of styles that will make a CV effective

▌ Understand the key messages that need to be communicated if you hope to get near a short list

"Embrace your uniqueness. Time is much too short to be living someone else's life."

Kobi Yamada

MATCHING YOUR CV TO YOUR PARTICULAR CIRCUMSTANCES

Chapter 5 will help you to think about the right style and format for your CV, but before you begin writing it's important to think about what you want your CV to achieve. Or, to put it another way: *what problem is your CV trying to solve?*

Horses for courses

Beware any guide that suggests there is a perfect CV. There isn't. At best, you'll come up with strong CV which will achieve four goals. It communicates your background. It matches your need to make a change.

It contains a clear, memorable message that will provoke a response in your target readership. And, finally, it will lead to the right action (typically, getting you a place on an interview shortlist).

What kind of CV will work for me? is not an easy question to solve – your age, your background and your target sector are all important variables. The best answer is always to find out what a winning CV looks like as far as your likely employer is concerned. Employer websites will sometimes give you this information, but you'll get equally good views from work colleagues and recruiters. Find out what your target employer likes to see in terms of key messages, and make sure they are all communicated on the first page of your CV as far as possible.

Don't make the mistake of choosing a CV format (a) because it looks easy or (b) because it's close to a format you've already used in the past. Often the best plan is to forget earlier drafts and start from scratch.

Elements which should be in any kind of CV

Format and Style: It will be rare that your CV needs to be longer than two pages, but, if it does, make sure the key information is on page 1.

Main Emphasis: Your CV will always include information about your main **skills**, how you present them will vary, but they should appear on the first page of your CV. The emphasis you give to **qualifications** will also vary. Always include **full contact details**, including an email address that you check regularly. When giving details of your **work experience**, there is evidence that mentioning **well-known companies or organisations** often helps gain credibility. As you go through your work history, job by job, make sure that you spell out details of your **skills**, acquired knowledge and – most importantly – **key achievements**. Keep personal information to a minimum, but say something engaging about your **interests**, ideally ensuring that they include at least one of the following: team work, community involvement, intellectual challenge. See Chapter 10 for more detailed advice on completing the various standard parts of your CV. Remember, too, that a strong **covering letter** will assist any kind of CV – as Chapter 13 reveals.

MATCHING YOUR CV TO THE KIND OF CHANGE YOU MIGHT WANT TO MAKE

The list below is not exhaustive, but gives you some tips on the style and format that will probably be appropriate for each of a range of staring points.

School leaver CV

Format and Style: This CV may not need to be much longer than a single page. Begin with **full contact details**, a **skills summary**, details of your **qualifications** (with grades), then your **work experience** (any kind of work), then any other kind of relevant experience, including volunteering, then include **interests**.

Main Emphasis: Most school leaver CVs place the main focus on educational history. Your **qualifications** are important, but make sure that **work experience** and **skills** also get onto the first page. Lead with a **profile** or a **summary of skills**. Mention any particular awards or **achievements** with a brief explanation if this is required. Emphasise any skills acquired in your studies, on work experience or in extracurricular activities (give particular emphasis to team working if you can). Refer to non-academic activities and interests.

College or university leaver CV

Format and Style: Two pages will probably be necessary. After **full contact details**, if you include a **profile** (see Chapters 7 and 8) use the word "graduate", "qualified" or similar – do this and you can leave your main qualification until lower on page 1.

Main Emphasis: List your main **qualifications** (if you have a degree, you probably don't need to list your GCSEs, unless you know that certain GCSEs such as Maths and English are required). Do make sure you include your class of degree or other examination results at the same level. When outlining your qualifications, translate them into terms that the reader will understand (drawing out your transferable skills).

List your **work experience**, briefly covering all temporary jobs, vacation jobs, work placements or internships. For each job, list the skills you used and, if possible, **achievements** – examples of where you made a difference. Make the main emphasis your skills and enthusiasm to learn. Make sure you include **interests**, as they will often communicate a rounder picture. Avoid making this CV look like the qualifications-led CV outlined in Chapter 5 by making sure you emphasise your **skills** and (however limited) your **work experience** on page 1.

Seeking a job where you have little work experience

Format and Style: This CV may well work in a single page format. Follow the same broad format as the school leaver CV.

Main Emphasis: Focus on what you can do, rather than what you can't. Work with a friend to draw out evidence of your skills, from any part of your life. Capture skills acquired from your hobbies or interests outside work. List any kind of **work experience**, including temporary work, voluntary work, vacation jobs or work placements. Don't oversell your skills, but don't miss them out either. If your CV states your target job, don't be unrealistic.

Seeking an internship or short-term assignment (paid or unpaid)

Format and Style: A one-page CV can work here. Again, a **profile** will probably help summarise the key information required to get your message across.

Main Emphasis: The simple question here is "why you?". Most others applying for the same internship will have achieved qualifications on a par with your own. Think about two main messages: What makes you suitable, and what attracts you. After **full contact details**, give major emphasis to a **skills summary** and a list of **achievements**. Spell out, in a covering letter if necessary, why you want to gain experience in this sector and this organisation (this means you have to do your homework as far as research is concerned).

New sector, second job after graduating

Format and Style: This CV needs to be brief, once again, and certainly no more than two pages. The format depends on whether you want to change sector or carry on along the same path (see Chapter 5). The likelihood is that you will probably be using a variant on the **"straight-in" CV**. However, if there is no obvious link between your degree subject and your first job then a **profile** may have to do a great deal of the work here. Make sure it shows the link between your studies, your previous experience, your present job, and your ideal next role.

Main Emphasis: Include **full contact details**, a **set of bullet points listing key experiences and achievements**, then give plenty of details about what you have achieved in your first job. Move on to your previous **work experience**, then a short summary of your **qualifications**, then details of your **interests**.

Same sector, second job after graduating

Format and Style: Two pages again, with a format as follows: should be: **full contact details**, possibly a **set of bullet points listing key experiences and achievements**, details of your first job, including linked **achievements** and previous **work experience**, then a short summary of your **qualifications**, then details of your **interests**.

Main Emphasis: If you state a target job, make sure it's not over-ambitious. If you're after the next obvious job, a **"straight-in" CV** may do the trick nicely (see Chapter 6). Again, give plenty of emphasis to transferable skills and achievements.

Staying in the same sector, but moving on to a more demanding or interesting job in your chosen field or seeking a promotion

Format and Style: The **"straight-in" CV** works best. This will probably be no more than two pages, structured in the following sequence: **full contact details**, possibly a **skill summary**, information about your **key**

experiences and achievements, job-by-job **work experience, qualifications** and, finally, your **interests**.

Main Emphasis: A profile may be counterproductive here. The main focus is on your present and recent jobs. Make sure you explain what you bring to the party by including, against each job, bullet points listing **key experiences and achievements** that will provide plenty of evidence to get you shortlisted and a wealth of material at interview. If you are thinking of moving outside your present organisation make sure your **work experience** translates easily to another employer.

With work experience and just concluded an **MBA** or some other professional qualification

Format and Style: This needs to have a clear emphasis on the different stages in your career and your reasons for study. This should be spelt out in your **profile** or in your list of jobs and experiences. You will almost certainly wish to go for a **"profile-led" CV** (see Chapter 7).

Main Emphasis: Your most recent **qualification** is part of your main message, but not the whole deal. The primary message in the first two-thirds of page 1 of your profile-led CV needs to be about your reasons for gaining this significant qualification. Begin with **full contact details**, then add a well-written **profile** that explains briefly why you chose to study a MBA (or other professional qualification), what you learned from it and how you hope to apply it in your next role (or promotion). Reinforce this in your **skills summary** or **set of bullet points listing key experiences and achievements**. If you want to emphasis the breadth of your career, consider a **career summary**. Then give details of your various jobs, including linked **achievements** and previous **work experience**, then a short summary of your **qualifications**, then details of your **interests**.

After a long and difficult job search

Format and Style: The format of your CV will depend on whether your likely next role follows a predictable career path or you want to do something new.

Main Emphasis: Make sure that your primary message is **not** about your job search. Don't refer to any difficulties you have experienced, and don't draw immediate attention to the gap between today and your last work experience. The main focus should be your **skills summary**, your availability, and your **set of bullet points listing key experiences and achievements** – it may be the lack of such evidence in your CV that has failed to get you shortlisted. Draw out skills and motivation from your **work experience**. Your **interests** may need to give strong evidence of motivation if you are hoping to convince an employer that you haven't been entirely inactive.

Returning to work after a gap studying

Format and Style: Probably similar to the CV you would use if dealing with an MBA or other professional qualification (see above).

Main Emphasis: The main goal here is to communicate clear motivation behind your life decisions, particularly if (a) you took time off work to study and (b) your chosen area of study is not directly linked to your occupation. Highlight your transferable **skills** (possibly using a **profile** and **skills summary**), but remember that the reader needs more than anything else to know whether you are now firmly committed to a return to the kind of work on offer. Explain what you studied and what you got out of it.

Returning to work after a career break

Format and Style: Choose a format that very early on deals with the sequence of events, your life choices and where your career is heading next. This is probably best done with a well-crafted **profile** and **skills summary** where you say why you chose to take a career break, what barriers you had to overcome to make it happen and what you got out of it. In your **set of bullet points listing key experiences and achievements**, list the skills you used to arrange and experience your career break, and what you learned from this.

Main Emphasis: Employers are getting used to career breakers, and a person who actively manages their life and personal resources so that they can go off to do something exciting stands out from the crowd. Do remember that an employer is also wondering whether you are now fully committed to a return to a more "conventional" lifestyle, so emphasise your commitment.

Returning to work after a gap taken for personal or family reasons

Format and Style: Use the career break model above, and deal with the "personal issue" briefly.

Main Emphasis: Honesty is the best policy, but do give the emphasis to your transferable skills and your motivation to get back to work. If you have been away from work for more than 2 years or so, try to introduce evidence of skills you have exercised out of work in the intervening period (e.g. in voluntary work). Don't give the reader any indication that your skills are out of date (e.g. by putting dates against training courses you did some time back). If your reason for having a gap was to do with family responsibilities, be very clear about your current availability.

Wanting to stay in the same role but in a different sector

Format and Style: This CV probably needs to be **profile-led**. Emphasise your professional background *and* give a value reason for wanting to change sector, and say what experience, know-how and skills you want to bring across. You may find that the **one-page ad** version of the profile-led CV helps here (see Chapter 7).

Main Emphasis: Begin with **full contact details**. The art here is in writing a strong **profile**, but make sure that you bring relevant examples into your **work experience**. If you have spent a long time in one sector it is best to leave job-by-job details until page 2 or consider writing a

functional CV (see Chapter 5) to emphasise your skills more than the organisations you have worked for. However, you can often achieve the same impact with a well-constructed **set of bullet points listing key experiences and achievements**. Sectoral knowledge can be emphasised in the profile or possibly in a **career summary**. Again, refer to your **interests**, particularly if there is a link to the new sector.

Wanting to stay in the same sector but in a different role

Format and Style: Again, a **profile-led** format will probably be required, as here, once more, you have to sell a particular idea to a recruiter.

Main Emphasis: You will probably need to take the emphasis off your main **qualification** and your professional background. You may also find that it helps if you focus on relevant training. When discussing your **work experience** take the emphasis off your previous job titles. Consider using a **functional CV** (see Chapter 5). Major on transferable skills by selling appropriate stories in your **set of bullet points listing key experiences and achievements**. Include evidence from projects or placements where you have gone outside your job description. The biggest emphasis of all (probably in the **profile**, but consider a **career summary**) should be on (a) your in-depth knowledge of the sector and (b) your clearly articulated motivation to stay in the sector but in a new role.

Wanting to change role *and* sector – to do something completely new

Format and Style: This is the hardest kind of CV to write. You will probably want to take a **profile-led** approach (setting out your skills or competencies in a well-developed **set of bullet points listing key experiences and achievements**). The format is going to be very flexible, depending on what you are using the CV for and at which sector you are aiming. You may find that, because of the need to get across a very clear message, the **one-page ad** variant on the **profile-led CV** works well. Consider writing a **functional CV** (see Chapter 5) if your transferable skills are not immediately obvious from your job roles or work history.

Main Emphasis: As ever, begin with **full contact details**. Your **profile** has to work overtime here, spelling out your reasons for change, what attracts you to the new role and something of what you have to offer. Do give particular emphasis to (a) clarity of purpose and (b) saying something distinctive and unusual about your background – tickling the reader's curiosity is often what gets you through to a first interview. When setting out your **work experience** and **qualifications** do everything you can to point to transferable skills.

At the networking stage when you are still working out what you want to do, you're probably best using the "same sector but in a different role" CV covered above. As you become clearer about your target sector make your CV an increasingly focused profile-led or functional CV which makes it very clear what you have to offer your target field of work.

Applying for a role that has defined competencies

Format and Style: Your target employer may publish a list of detailed competencies for the job (see Chapter 12). You may find you need a more developed version of the functional CV – the **competency-led CV** (see Chapter 5).

Main Emphasis: After **full contact details** you will probably wish to move directly to a list of **competencies** drawn from your **work experience** (but also from study, personal interests, voluntary work or other life experiences). Don't omit your **qualifications and training** as they may also be required to get you shortlisted.

Wanting to communicate strong personal beliefs or unusual interests

Format and Style: If you find that you really want to write this CV, bring the **interests** section forward to page 1. However, see below.

Main Emphasis: Whether you're determined to write about your two unpublished novels, your lifelong passion for growing orchids, your new-found religious conviction or your allegiance to a political cause, your CV is not the right place to mention it unless it makes sense to the job. Recruiters and employers get very nervous indeed about statements of this kind – largely because they see what you say in very one-dimensional terms. Many of my clients have found that a statement of personal faith on a CV often leads to wrong assumptions about a whole host of things from commitment levels to the assumption that you hold hard-line views that will upset your work colleagues.

Wanting to get into a new, highly competitive sector

Format and Style: This CV needs to be no longer than two pages, with a clear answer to the message "why you?" on page 1. A **profile-led CV** may work, but do respond to what recruitment consultants want to see: if your experience fits the format, go with the **"straight-in" CV**.

Main Emphasis: Get your **key experiences and achievements** right and you have half a chance of getting shortlisted. Anything that is predictable, ordinary or overblown will get you excluded, but something distinctive and unusual (including multi-sector experience or a career break) might get you noticed. Do remember that a strong CV alone is unlikely to create the outcome you want – it needs to be linked to a multi-strategy career-exploration and job-search plan (see Chapter 11).

Trying to get an interview for a job where you have little obvious experience

Format and Style: **Profile-led**, with particular emphasis as below.

Main Emphasis: Take the emphasis off your **work experience** and particularly your previous job titles – keep this information on page 2 or consider writing a **functional CV**. Your **profile** and your **set of bullet points listing key experiences and achievements** have to do all the work here. If you can convince a reader to give you an interview it will be because you have really explained and sold your transferable skills. Make sure your **profile** gives a clear, motivated reason for wanting to make this kind of move. A **career summary** might help bring out useful background jobs. The odds are long on this kind of application, but if you can get into the interview room you have a chance.

Age 50+ and finding it hard to get an interview

Format and Style: The standard **profile-led** format is the best starting point – if your CV looks smart and modern that will help. Include an email address. Don't provide endless information about jobs you did over 15 years ago in the **work experience** section.

Main Emphasis: You might assume that the age discrimination law in the UK means that the over-50s no longer have to worry about getting through to interview. There is plenty of evidence to the contrary. This CV needs to major on up-to-date transferable skills and recent evidence of achievement. Get a younger colleague to check the language – are you using terminology that a 25-year-old recruiter would find archaic? List recent jobs and don't put dates against work experience, qualifications or training that will give the impression that your skills are rusty. Don't include your date of birth, the age of your children or anything else that overemphasises age. For the same reason, you may want to avoid a career summary as it may overemphasise your length of service. Do include recent projects and consultancy assignments if you've been out of work for a while.

Wanting to find a permanent job after a series of temporary positions

Format and Style: Use the **profile-led** format, giving emphasis to the broad range of skills and experience you have achieved. If you simply list your temporary jobs in a **"straight-in"** format you will simply communicate a message that you are looking for another temporary role.

Main Emphasis: In both the **profile** and the **set of bullet points listing key experiences and achievements** bring out the breadth of your **work experience** – you will probably have experience of a wider range of organisations than many people who have been in the same role for a number of years, and you should be able to point to a good range of transferable skills. The problem is that your CV can look very transitory, and can be mistaken for the CV of someone looking for another temporary job. A **profile** and lists of skills and achievements can help to summarise fragmentary information. Don't be afraid of including the phrase "permanent role" in your target job statement.

Looking for a temporary or contract job

Format and Style: A one-page CV may be all you need here. Don't worry about the profile or the complications of communicating the idea that you want a permanent job. An agency needs to see (a) a **skills summary**, (b) a list of **roles and organisations** for the last 2–3 years and (c) your main offerings in terms of **qualifications** and training.

Main Emphasis: If you are looking for a temporary position you are probably approaching employment agencies specialising in this service. **Skills** and **achievements** are everything – an agency wants to know if you can hit the deck running. An indication of availability is often also welcome – how far are you prepared to travel and how soon could you start a new assignment?

Looking for work as an interim manager

Format and Style: Interim managers are typically hired to cover relatively senior positions for anything between a month and a year. A proven track record in a particular sector is going to be a must, so a **"straight-in" CV** is probably going to be required. Aim for no more than three pages unless you are adding case studies (developed histories of previous interim positions). An interim management agency will usually need to see a fully developed list of **skills**, and clear reference to earlier roles and organisations (a **career summary** may help).

Main Emphasis: Outline the results you have achieved in previous roles, giving greater attention to your **achievements** in the last 3–4 years as interim managers are hired for their current knowledge. In particular, highlight any projects undertaken in previous jobs. Emphasise project management or change management. Include as many relevant keywords as possible that would be required by your specialist area. An indication of availability is also sometimes useful.

Seeking an internship or work placement (paid or unpaid)

Format and Style: This CV (perhaps restricted to one page) will probably be accompanied by a strong **covering letter**. A **profile** may be useful for reinforcing, in a nutshell, how such an experience will assist you in your career.

Main Emphasis: The reader is going to spend less time considering this application than for a permanent job, so focus on three main messages: (1) why you want the experience, (2) what you want to get out of it and (3) what you will bring to the party. Cover all three in your **covering letter**, and then make sure that your **profile** and **set of bullet points listing key experiences and achievements** match.

Wanting to be a self-employed consultant

Format and Style: Here you need a one-page CV that is more like a business flier. It may look quite like the first page of a **profile-led** CV (particularly the **one-page ad** variant outlined in Chapter 7).

Main Emphasis: Your **full contact details** may include a business name. You may start with a **profile**, but this may be more of a branding statement about what you do and what sets you apart from the competition. Instead of listing your key experience and achievements, provide a list of recent projects (stating the organisation, the nature of the project and the outcome). A short **career summary** including job titles and names of organisations may be more appropriate than a detailed job-by-job listing as far as your **work experience** is concerned.

Wanting to undertake a mix of part-time, voluntary and assignment work (i.e. a portfolio career)

Format and Style: Depending on your background, a range of CV formats will work as long as there is a clear message in your **profile** that indicates how your background and experience knit together. You may only need a summary of your **work experience** and **qualifications**.

Main Emphasis: Instead of a conventional **set of bullet points listing key experiences and achievements**, your portfolio CV will probably set out not only your skills and recent projects, but will also detail the current range of projects with which you have recently been involved.

What next?

Once you've worked out what problem your CV is trying to solve, you need to begin to think about how you are going to customise it to your needs. Part 2 of this book helps you to make a final decision if you can't decide whether to lead with a profile or not, and goes on to assist with the toughest question of all – what are you going to say?

Choosing the Right Format

CHAPTER 5

This chapter helps you to:

I Avoid conventional CV structures that fail to work

I Choose between different CV formats

I See the advantages and disadvantages of different models

I Anticipate the impact of different CVs on recruiters

"Form follows function."

Louis Henri Sullivan (American architect)

FORMATS TO AVOID

By this point you've thought about what you're up against, and you know what kind of results you want to get from your CV. Before you begin writing, you need to think about choosing the right format. We begin by looking at two formats that fail to impress because their emphasis is all in the wrong place – the biographical CV and the qualifications-led CV.

One to avoid: the biographical CV

This form of CV is the most widely used, and the easiest to write – you may have used it yourself in the past. Recruiters complain that they see them all the time, from candidates at all levels, but particularly by recent graduates and school leavers or those who have been out of the labour market for some time. It looks rather like this.

Format of the biographical CV

Name	LATEST JOB
Address	Responsibilities listed
Contact details	_____
PERSONAL INFORMATION	_____
Date of birth	_____
Marital status	_____
Ages of children	_____
Driving licence	
Nationality	PREVIOUS JOBS
Health information	_____
	_____
QUALIFICATIONS	_____
Names of schools attended _____	_____
All qualifications listed _____	_____
	_____
	_____
TRAINING	
All courses listed _____	REFERENCES
_____	_____
	_____
HOBBIES AND INTERESTS	_____
_____	_____
_____	_____
_____	_____
1	2

This CV format, once very popular, has few advantages – it does at least show that you have a life outside work. However, the CV is upside down – job information is hidden away on page 2 (and skills may not be brought out at all). The initial information provided may be distracting – information about your family, background, hobbies and qualifications can encourage all kinds of unhelpful stereotyping. Most of the information is irrelevant, creating irritation in the reader. The CV fails to write about transferable skills. Worse still, the CV gives no sense of direction or purpose – what kind of job are you after?

If you're determined **not** to get a job interview and to be excluded with a pile of similarly undifferentiated messages, the biographical CV will do the trick.

Another weak format: the qualifications-led CV

The qualifications-led CV is a variation on the biographical CV. This kind of CV is often used by recent college and university leavers. CVs of this kind land on recruiters' desks every day – and quickly go onto the "no" pile. Ironically, although these CVs are written by people who are keen to gain work experience, their primary message is the thing that has been most recent and relevant to them – getting qualified.

Format of the qualifications-led CV

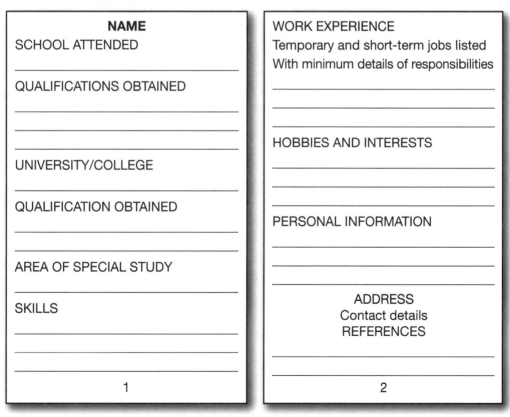

Why a Qualifications-led CV Creates Problems

1. The first thing the reader encounters is your school. Trying to impress? This is very hit and miss, whether you went to Eton or Slackville High. You are inviting the reader to jump to all kinds of unhelpful conclusions.

2. Next, the reader has to deal with your most recent qualification – if this isn't directly a match for the job, you're already risking a "no".

3. The CV draws attention to your qualifications above everything else, prompting all kinds of unhelpful questions: e.g. "is this candidate over- or underqualified?", "does this candidate have any work experience?".

4. If you've studied more than one subject, you may communicate confused objectives.

5. The biggest problem with this format is that much of the relevant information about your skills and capability is at the bottom of page 1 or on page 2 – assuming that you do more than present a chopped-up job description, which most candidates don't. A busy recruiter will probably look no further than your primary qualifications plus your most recent job title.

The obvious question is this: how do you avoid writing a qualifications-led CV if you have just qualified? The key thing is to put as much skills-related information on page 1 as you possibly can, even if those skills were acquired in temporary or holiday jobs, on a work placement or in your studies. Making the reader plough through a long list of your educational history and qualifications really sends a message "I have no experience, but great potential".

Doesn't that message work, sometimes? We all know young people who get interesting jobs. But look again at their CV or interview performance. Somewhere – usually in extra-curricular experiences – the big question "why you?" has been answered. For this reason, almost anything you can say about your know-how and abilities above and beyond your list of qualifications is helpful (see Chapter 3 for more on this issue).

Advantages of the qualifications-led CV	Disadvantages
• It may be useful if you want to go on to do further study	• You start by presenting distracting information about your schooling
• It may form the basis for a CV seeking an academic position (it will also need to list publications and areas of research)	• Your main qualification becomes the main subject of the CV – not much use if your qualification is not closely linked to a particular career or if you want to change careers
• If you need a specific qualification for a job this will be clear.	• The CV is upside down – job information is hidden away on page 2
	• Skills evidence is often difficult to identify.

CV FORMATS THAT DO WORK

Although there are many variations and hybrids, there are essentially three formats that do have a chance of working, depending on your needs (see Chapter 4) – the "straight-in" CV, the profile-led CV and the functional CV.

THE "STRAIGHT-IN" CV

The "straight-in" CV is so called because it goes directly into the details of your latest role. This CV is reverse chronological (i.e. your most recent job appears first). It begins with full contact details, then a detailed overview of your present (or most recent) job. After that it works backwards, one job at a time. The net result is that your current skills and work focus are the main story on page 1 of your CV.

Format of the "straight-in" CV

Name
Address
Contact Details

Latest Job
Overview of the role and organisation
_____
_____
_____

Key achievements: _____
_____
_____
_____
_____

Previous Job
Overview of the role and organisation
_____
_____

Key achievements: _____
_____
_____
_____
_____

1

Previous Job
Overview of the role and organisation
_____
_____

Key achievements: _____
_____

Previous Job
Overview of the role and organisation
_____
_____

Key achievements: _____
_____

Qualifications
_____
_____

Training Courses Attended
_____
_____

Interests
_____
_____

2

The "straight-in" model is the very simplest form of CV, and one not to be disparaged. It is uncluttered, clear and useful if your next move is uncomplicated.

Stuart McIntosh, Managing Consultant of CMC's northern offices, comments that "a straightforward, simple and honest reverse chronological CV, preferably without a profile, is the recommended option for those seeking a similar role in a similar sector. In the main, recruiters favour a no-nonsense, no bells and whistles approach to CVs, and unless you are seeking to reinvent yourself then simplest is best. They will probably go immediately to page 2 to look at your last one or two roles and employers before deciding whether to read the CV in detail. Make it easy for them and you stand a better chance of going into the 'yes' pile".

Steps to writing a "straight-in" CV

As with other CV models, you need to spend time analysing the skills you used in each job, and presenting matched achievements. The main message is in your current or, if you are between jobs, your most recent job. How you describe this role (name of organisation, job title, outlined responsibilities) is crucial. It is also vital that you give close attention to discussing not just your responsibilities and work experience, but also to spell out your **achievements** – otherwise your CV ends up as a chopped-up version of your job description.

In the "straight-in" CV your latest job, and how you describe it, is the key ingredient because you are relying on getting a decision to interview you based on a very quick read largely of this information alone. This initial decision needs to be supported by other key facts, which again are easily visible: any key qualifications, training received, previous role titles and the names of former employers.

Chapter 6 provides a detailed explanation of how to write a "straight-in" CV.

Advantages of the "straight-in" CV	Disadvantages
• It gets immediately to your most recent job – assuming that this is your main selling point	• If you fail to translate job responsibilities into active information about skills and achievements the CV will be as ineffective as a biographical CV
• It is popular with recruitment consultants	
• Your CV will almost certainly be no longer than two pages	• You may be pigeon-holed into an identical job to the one you have just done, with little opportunity for new learning
• Jobs are presented in a clear order	

Advantages of the "straight-in" CV	Disadvantages
• It is clear which skills you used in a particular job.	• If you have had a variety of jobs it may not be clear what you want to do next (in which case try a **profile-led CV**).

"Straight-in" CV benefits

When should you use the "straight-in" CV? This CV works well if you are simply looking for the next, fairly obvious role in your present sector. It's a no-brainer, no-fuss approach that says "this is what I do know, and I am in the market for the next job up the ladder". The fact that it is "straight-in" makes it popular with recruiters; however, it's also the kind of CV you might put together if you are seeking a promotion in your current department or function.

The "straight-in" CV does not use a profile because its main selling point is what you have done in your current or most recent job. You will quickly get a sense of whether your CV is working by the reaction of recruitment consultants – ask any agencies you are dealing with to summarise the kind of job they are trying to find for you based on your work history, and if you like the answer then your "straight-in" CV is doing the job.

However, the role that seems obvious to a recruiter might, in fact, not be right for you. You might not want a promotion or more responsibility. You might want a sideways move to gain different experience. You might want to do the same role with an organisation that has alternative values or a different culture. You might be seeking a particular kind of learning opportunity. If this is the case, the chances are that you will feel that a recruiter is misreading you or trying to put a square peg in a round hole. If this is the case, you might want to bring out different messages on the first page of your "straight-in" CV or you might, in fact, want to try the profile-led approach (see below).

THE PROFILE-LED CV

We now turn to a CV format that, although less popular with recruiters, is generally acceptable among HR departments and employers (as Chapter 2 demonstrates) – the **profile-led CV**. This CV starts, as the name indicates, with a short profile, and also presents other summary information on page 1. This will almost certainly include a list of key achievements. Page 1 may also mention your qualifications, training and a summary of your career to date.

The profile-led CV is useful for candidates who:

- Want to change sector *and* role.
- Want to stay in the same role but a different sector.
- Want to keep their options open.
- Have a varied employment history.
- Have taken a break, to study or for other reasons.
- Find that their CV results in offers of jobs identical to their present one.

The profile-led CV is far harder to write than a "straight-in" CV because it begins with a demanding piece of text – a short paragraph summarising who and what you are (see Chapter 8 for a lot more information about writing a strong CV profile). A typical opening profile might look something like this.

Profile

A versatile Chartered Chemical Engineer and Manager with experience in a wide range of technical, operational and leadership roles. A strong track record of project management including commissioning and managing a new plant, with a sound technical understanding of all areas of process plant design and operation. In-depth understanding of Health, Safety & Environmental legislation and responsibilities. Well-developed management and influencing skills with a history of leading effective teams.

Format of a profile-led CV

Name Address Contact Details **Profile** _____ _____ **Key Achievements** Theme 1: _____ _____ Theme 2: _____ _____ Theme 3: _____ _____ **Latest Job** Overview of the role and organisation _____ _____ Key achievements: _____ _____ _____ _____ _____ 1	**Previous Job** Overview of the role and organisation _____ _____ Key achievements: _____ _____ **Previous Job** Overview of the role and organisation _____ _____ Key achievements: _____ _____ **Qualifications** _____ _____ **Training Courses Attended** _____ _____ **Interests** _____ _____ 2

Steps to writing a profile-led CV

The key to writing a profile-led CV is to begin with the information required for the "straight-in" CV. It's usually impossible to write the profile first, as this summarises what you have done, and first of all you need to look at each job you have undertaken. So, start by analysing each job so that each one can be presented as follows.

Example of how to write about a job in a CV ("straight-in" or profile-led)

Senior Editor   Magic X Publications, Milton Keynes   2000–2004

Magic X is the UK's largest publisher of self-help books focused on the magic/conjurer sector. The Senior Editor is responsible for editing the monthly magazine *Magic Matters* (circulation 15,000) and a number of annual booklets

Key Achievements

- Improving circulation from 3,000 to 15,000 in 2 years

- Renegotiating printer contracts to save production costs

- Improving advertising income by 50%

- Securing monthly articles from leading British conjurors

- Attracting media interest, including a profile of the magazine on Switch TV's "Look Out", November 2003.

From this you can proceed to finalising a list of achievements on page 1 (see Chapter 9) and then to the profile (see Chapter 8).

Advantages of the profile-led CV	Disadvantages
• Your CV begins with a paragraph that summarises who you are and what you have to offer	• Profiles are not always popular with recruiters
• The profile may include evidence about what makes you distinctive	• If badly written, the profile sets a poor tone for the whole CV
• If you have had a variety of jobs it becomes easier to focus on what you want to do next	• If you have had a variety of jobs it's not clear what you want to do next
• Your most recent job can still be spotted quickly.	• You may run out of space for job information on page 1
	• Achievements may become disconnected from the jobs to which they relate.

See Chapter 7 for a detailed explanation of how to write a profile-led CV .

THE FUNCTIONAL CV

If you have a ever tried to move from one sector to another, you may have been recommended to write a functional CV. This is, essentially, a variation on the profile-led approach. It puts the spotlight not just on your work history but on your specific skills, sometimes closely matching that list to a target job. See below for an example.

Format of a functional CV

Name Address Contact Details **Profile** _____ _____ **Skill 1** Examples of how I used this skill: _____ _____ **Skill 2** Examples of how I used this skill: _____ _____ **Skill 3** Examples of how I used this skill: _____ **Skill 4** Examples of how I used this skill: _____ 1	**Skill 5** Examples of how I used this skill: _____ **Career History** Job & Responsibilities _____ Job & Responsibilities _____ Job & Responsibilities _____ Job & Responsibilities _____ Job & Responsibilities _____ **Training Courses Attended** _____ **Qualifications** _____ **Interests** _____ 2

Steps to writing a functional CV

A functional CV will usually begin with a profile, and then go on to discuss a number of specific skills. The main focus of page 1 of your CV now becomes a list of your key skills. If you know that your target employer normally recruits against a list of competency statements, you can adapt a functional CV to that purpose (discussed in the paragraphs below). The way skills are set out in a functional CV is shown below.

Example of page 1 of a functional CV

Name
Contact details

Profile
A results-focused graduate professional with a history of success in initiating and guiding projects, event management and creating measurable improvements in customer service standards. With extensive experience of liaison with a range of external partners in both the private and public sector, now seeking a business development role in a flexible, forward-looking organisation.

Business Development Skills
I have built strong relationships with key accounts, solving quality and ordering problems, and adding extra value. This has resulted in a 27% increase in orders into my department, and four major new external customers won in the last 18 months.

Planning Skills
I planned, organised and hosted a regional conference for 200 colleagues. This involved planning the programme, booking speakers and the venue, and organising invitation letters, delegate packs and follow-up documentation.

Customer Care Skills
Using highly developed customer-facing skills, I have been responsible for handling customer complaints to our department and have also planned a proactive programme of client consultation to gather information about the level of customer satisfaction in our top 40 users. As a result I designed and wrote a new customer service handbook.

Budgetary Management
I have had responsibility for setting and agreeing departmental budgets and reporting on actual versus budget costs on a monthly basis.

The material in the above page still focuses carefully on hard evidence of achievement, but instead of using each job as a heading the writer has chosen to list a number of skills. The CV is for someone who wants to move from a public sector service role into a private sector sales position. As a result, she is trying to overcome her lack of private sector experience by pointing, with strong supporting examples, to the fact that she possesses skills that are vital to the new role, e.g. business development, customer care and budgetary management skills. She has also been careful to adopt private sector terms, e.g. "accounts", "customers", "orders" rather than "partners" and "contracts".

The functional CV therefore works rather like the profile-led CV, except that it leads with a list of skills and communicates the fact that they are transferable. It also includes the kind of linked achievements that will be meaningful to an employer in a new sector. You will find it particularly useful to use the **Role Analysis Sheet** in Chapter 6, and also to look at Chapter 9 for ways of drawing out your skills and achievements.

Competency statements in a functional CV

You can also adapt a functional CV to cover not just skills, but competency statements (see Chapter 12 for more details of competency-based selection). To write about a competency is to write about more than skills, but also to say something about underpinning knowledge, how and where you used the skill, and at what level.

A competency-statement CV (effectively a variation on the functional CV) is again structured not around your chronological work history but around your primary competencies, which are usually matched very closely to your typical target job. As the main function of a competency statement CV is to communicate evidence that you match the competencies for the job, a profile may not be required. A competency statement in a CV will look something like this.

> **Leading and motivating teams**
>
> *A confident, energetic, leadership style that values genuine consultation but also offers clarity of direction (evidenced by repeated 360 degree feedback). A track record of motivating teams to set and achieve demanding goals under pressure.*

Do note, however, that for some jobs, including senior jobs, this approach may appear too gimmicky. It may be best to outline relevant competencies in a covering letter.

Advantages of the functional CV (using either skill or competency statements)	Disadvantages
• Your CV begins by focusing on what you can do; this skills evidence can make you distinctive	• Functional CVs are often unpopular with recruitment consultants, who feel that job information is concealed
• If you have had a variety of jobs it becomes easier to focus on your transferable skills	• If badly written, the skills list sets a poor tone for the whole CV
• It can be adapted to refer to competencies	• If you pick the wrong skills or describe them in a way that doesn't match the job, the chances of selection are slim
• Some employers are more influenced by clear competency statements (less so for more senior jobs)	• Information about your job history is still hidden on page 2
• The CV matches the typical shopping list of your target employer.	• If you pick the wrong skills/competencies, or describe them at the wrong level, your chances are reduced.

IN A HURRY? HOW TO DECIDE ON THE FORMAT THAT WORKS FOR YOU

Having looked at the major species of CV you will find in the wild, you will already have come to the conclusion that, from an end-user point of view, there are clear favourites. Deciding which CV format to use is relatively straightforward:

- If your need is simple, to move a step up the ladder in the sector of your choice, go for a **"straight-in" CV**.

- If in doubt, it's because you don't know exactly what to go for. In this case, a variation on the **profile-led CV** is going to work for you.

- Even if you have only just left full-time education, don't get bogged down by a qualifications-led CV. Use a **profile-led CV** or **"straight-in" CV** to give as much emphasis as possible to your skills.

- If you're finding it hard to change sectors, consider a **functional CV**.

- If you are trying to match specific competencies in a job, consider using a **competency-based CV** or at least consider using the list of competencies on page 1 of a profile-led CV.

Cutting to the Chase: The "Straight-in" CV

This chapter helps you to:

I Gain the greatest benefits from the "straight-in" CV model

I Provide credible back-up details about your work history

I Understand how to communicate your strengths on paper

I Communicate evidence as well as claims

"This report, by its very length, defends itself against the risk of being read."

Winston Churchill

BEGINNING TO WRITE A "STRAIGHT-IN" CV
Format of the "straight-in" CV

We have already seen the "straight-in" CV in outline form in Chapter 5 (see page 64). The following draft "straight-in" CV was written by someone seeking a role in a bigger organisation. It clearly communicates skills and experience. With a good covering letter to a recruiter (which says a little more about the ideal next role) this CV will serve its purpose well. Note that this CV has been abbreviated to fit on the page – you can, of course, get in rather more text than this on each A4 page and still have plenty of white space:

Example "straight-in" CV (page 1)

> No profile, but straight in to your work history. Use clear headings for each section, with the keywords on the left-hand side of the page

> Clear opening sets out your contact details including an email address

Jane Smith

12 Dungaree Close, Upper Boxton, Newbold
Cheshire CN1 2AA
Home tel 01234 987654   Mob 07777 987654   email jane@example.net

> Start with you latest job. Outline the organisation and role, showing how your job fits in

ASSISTANT MANAGER   LEMON TREE PROMOTIONS   2004–PRESENT

Lemon Tree is a direct mail organisation based in the North West importing and selling high-quality aromatherapy and related products. The role involves managing all sales enquiries from the Northern region, managing a team of seven staff and supervising the development of Lemon Tree's website.

Key Achievements and Experience

> Use high-energy language in your bullet points

- Direct mail experience – personal responsibility for 2007 campaign reaching 55,000 customers

- Deputising for Managing Director at key meetings with suppliers

- Negotiating with overseas suppliers to obtain quality product at the right price

- Commissioning a new website in 2005, with a resulting 60% increase in web-based turnover

- Supervising, challenging and motivating a telephone sales team

- Recruiting effective sales staff (with measurable improvements in staff retention)

- Making key contributions at sales strategy meetings

- Researching good practice by undertaking a work placement at BB Direct Mail

- Making recommendations regarding product range

> Don't leave big gaps between section headings and following text

> Lead with job title on left, followed by organisation name, location and years employed

SALES TEAM LEADER   LEMON TREE PROMOTIONS   2001–2004

The role involved dealing with sales enquiries, obtaining contact details, gaining commitment and closing sales generated through the Lemon Tree website.

Key Achievements and Experience

- Handling sales calls on new products, contributing to a 12% growth in profitability in 2003/04

- Dealing with customer complaints

- Training new and temporary members of the telephone sales team

- Keeping sales records

- Making suggestions regarding web site development (which led to my promotion to the role of Assistant Manager)

....

Example "straight-in" CV (page 2)

> Continue on page 2 with your work history, using a more edited approach

CUSTOMER SERVICES ASSISTANT   NW ELECTRICALS   2000–2001

NW Electricals is a wholesale organisation supplying electrical goods and components to retailers and independent traders/electricians.

Key Achievements and Experience

> Include key achievements for at least one job on page 2

- Receiving and handling sales enquiries on the full range of products

- Handling and resolving customer complaints

- Contributing to a staff-training handbook in telephone sales

- Providing weekly statistical reports to the department manager

SALES ASSISTANT   **ACE FASHION**   **1998–2000**

Working as a sales assistant in a busy retail environment gave me a good grounding in understanding and anticipating customer expectations and providing a high standard of service.

> Jobs you did some time ago can be summarised briefly

SALES ASSISTANT   **PCW STATIONERY, DERBY**   **1998**

Part-time Sales Assistant at a busy stationery and office supplies store.

> List any qualifications which confirm your thinking and learning ability

QUALIFICATIONS AND PROFESSIONAL TRAINING

- **Negotiating Skills** – ABC Foundation (2 days)   2007

- **NFC Customer Care programme** – (2 days plus follow up)   2005
  (introduced me to objective measures of raised customer satisfaction)

- **3 'A' Levels** – Information Technology (C), English Literature (C), History (D)

- **8 GCSEs** grade C and above including English, Mathematics and Science

> Mention training (including courses that did not lead to a certificate) as well as qualifications. Lead with the main focus of the training event on the left-hand side

INTERESTS

Keen swimmer with bronze and silver ASA life-saving awards.

Assistant group leader with 5th Newtown Scouts.

> Mention any interests that communicate skills (particularly team working), motivation or initiative

ANALYSING PAST JOBS

Before committing ideas to paper, try using the **Role Analysis Sheet** below. Complete one sheet for each role you intend to discuss in detail in your CV.

Role Analysis Sheet

Job Title:	
Dates of starting and finishing	
Main areas of responsibility when I started the job	
Additional areas of responsibility acquired while doing the job	
New skills acquired (with examples of where skills were used)	
Previous skills developed (with examples)	
Training received while doing this job	
Qualifications acquired while doing this job	
Projects I initiated personally	
New ideas I introduced or implemented	
Activities where I received positive feedback from my boss/colleagues/customers	
Examples of where I increased sales or profits or improved productivity	
Examples of where I saved costs	
Examples of where I provided excellent customer service	
Other areas where I added value or made a difference	

MAKING THE MOST OF A "STRAIGHT-IN" CV

As our example shows, what the "straight-in" CV offers is a detailed list of key achievements in your last one or two roles. Don't feel too constrained by the heading: you might equally use "key experience and achievements" or "key areas of experience". It's up to you – not all roles sit comfortably with the idea of achievement.

Using the Role Analysis Sheet to write your CV

You will find it useful to complete an A4 version of the Role Analysis Sheet for each of the jobs you wish to detail in your CV.

As you fill in the Role Analysis Sheet ensure you include plenty of examples, even if you only use bullet points to remind you of particular occasions. Don't worry if there are blanks or gaps – the sheet is simply there as a memory prompt. You'll discover that everything from the second line down provides you with information about what you actually did. Don't rely on memory – using an exercise like this or talking a role through with a friend is a necessary memory-jogger to help you recover key evidence.

Once you have completed an analysis sheet for each key role, start to transfer information to the CV in bullet-point form, keeping the information as brief and factual as possible. Where possible, make reference to tangible outcomes. See Chapter 9 for more information on communicating achievements.

You may find the Role Analysis Sheet a useful exercise for career development and job interviews, so hang on to this information for future use.

The main effect of discussing your work experience is to provide credible detail about *what you have actually done*. Too many CVs fail to do this, and end up providing rehashed job descriptions. A recruiter isn't interested in the basics of the job, but in what you did to add value, and especially in what you did to change the role and make a contribution to the organisation.

Writing about jobs you did before your latest one

Capturing your work history on paper is a process of processing, filtering and editing your experience so that it makes sense to a recruiter or employer. Whatever CV format you choose, it's best to begin with your current or more recent role. Having said that, it's often easier to start writing about jobs you did some time ago. Try writing page 2 of your CV first, covering the jobs that require only outline information first (like Jane Smith's retail jobs in our example CV), and then look in a lot more detail at the jobs you are covering on page 1.

When summarising a job, begin by stating the dates that you worked for an employer, the organisation's name and your job title. Also, mention the location of the employer (not the full address). Put these into a header, in a single line, in bold print, as shown in the example of Jane Smith's CV. If it's not clear from the organisation name what, exactly, your employer does, find some way of spelling this out briefly. Summarise the role and the organisation as quickly as possible, ideally in no more than two lines of text, e.g.:

1999–2002   Distribution Manager   Abstract Cartons, Nottingham

Abstract supplies pre-packaged cartons to the food sector. The Distribution Manager reports directly to the MD and has full responsibility for managing a transport pool and all daily deliveries in the East Midlands area.

Refer back to your **Role Analysis Sheet** for prompts. Simply listing jobs and outlining your responsibilities takes you as far as the average CV – a brief summary of the organisation and role. To make your CV stand out from the crowd, learn to dig deeper for the information that really matters. As you write your bullet points, think carefully about phrases that are going to be meaningful to the reader – what in your past is going to be useful currency with a new employer? You will see from the example set out below that only a small range of evidence will get as far as your CV:

> **1998–2001   Membership Team   Institute of Transport**
> **Leader   Professionals, Carlisle**
>
> *Head of team managing membership function for professional body with international reputation. Responsible for organising membership database and handling member enquiries.*
>
> ***Key Achievements:***
>
> - *Our team highlighted in the ITP Annual report for generating the largest number of innovations in 2000*
>
> - *Organised a switchover from a custom-designed system to a Windows-based network*
>
> - *Managed 7,500 member records, cross-checked for accuracy.*

What's different about the way you write about your latest job?

You will write about your current or most recent job in a lot more detail. You may want to say a little more in general about the organisation and the role than you have about previous jobs. Then move on to include at least five and as many as nine, bullet points covering your achievements. Consider breaking them down into sub-headings. For example:

Example of how to write about your latest job in your CV

> **2000–2002   Business Travel Consultant Acme   B2B Travel, London**
>
> *Acme B2B provides a bespoke travel service to the business community, specialising in media organisations. My role was based at the busy Heathrow branch.*
>
> ***Key Achievements and Experience:***
>
> **Organisation**
>
> - *Organised international travel arrangements for a variety of businesses.*
>
> - *Sole responsibility for planning 2006 Bejing Conference for Institute of Transport Professionals.*
>
> **Handling key customer accounts**
>
> - *Arranged bookings for large groups of news reporters and camera crews (often at very short notice and to specific budgets).*
>
> - *Managed to win a new contract with a major media group worth £120K per annum.*

> **Managing and Developing Others**
>
> • *Trained staff in telephone techniques and communication skills.*
>
> • *Designed and wrote staff induction manual.*

Where do achievements fit into a CV?

A good business report usually includes an executive summary. So, in the same way, a good CV may want to capture the key messages on page 1. This will be your choice if you decide to go for a profile-led CV (see Chapter 7). If you write a "straight-in" CV you will probably be listing key achievements after each job. In a functional CV (see Chapter 5) you will be linking achievements to skill headings.

Some recruiters don't like to see a list of achievements separated from job-by-job details. On the other hand, our research indicates that employers see them as a helpful summary. One HR manager pointed to the pleasing trend that recent CVs contain "more focus on achievements rather than duties alone".

Prompts to help you record "Key Achievements and Experience"

- Look at the Job Description for your last job. In what ways did you redefine the job?

- Go back through your work diaries and logs. Pick out occasions or projects where you made a difference.

- Spot the times when you, personally, did something. If you did it as part of a team, concentrate on what you added to the team (how would the team have been different if you hadn't been part of it?).

- When have you delivered more than was expected of you?

- Ask your colleagues and friends what differences you have made, and what you have added to organisations.

- Look for the right clues in your work history. There will be a problem or a set of obstacles, a challenge. You found some strategy for dealing with the problem – you sought help or you learned how to do something quickly.

- Spot the times when activities would have failed/lost money/faded away if you had not been there.

- Look at times when you invented new solutions, threw out the rule book, went the extra mile, gave 150%, came up with a surprising result … .

- Identify moments when you snatched victory from the jaws of failure.

- Remember to look at achievements in your non-working life. It's often here that you find skills that are undervalued or undeveloped.

- Try to express achievements in terms of concrete results, e.g. awards, money, time or percentages.

Writing the headlines in your story

Writing evidence of achievement in a CV is also fairly difficult to get right – but not if you know how. Imagine that you were writing a complete edition of a newspaper that was all about *you*. Deep inside you might have a lot of chatty personal material. On pages 2 and 3 of the newspaper you would probably have some detailed, extended stories about the work you have done. On page 1 of the newspaper you would have some headlines. Evidence from the newspaper industry shows that, on average, five times as many people read headlines as read the body of an article. So your headings and bullet points really matter. Page 1 of your CV is effectively a number of short, punchy articles with strong headlines. The first two-thirds of page 1 of your CV provides the main headline *and* lead story, swiftly followed by explanations and evidence. A CV without clear statements of achievement is not worth writing. It is this evidence in a CV that answers the question "what happened because *you* were in the job?.

In our CV survey one HR director indicated the importance of this area: "It is helpful that applicants point out strengths and achievements rather than leaving you trawling through everything and having to draw your own conclusions about what they may have achieved in a particular role".

You may feel uncomfortable writing about achievements through modesty or because you're working in a sector that avoids or disparages the language of achievement. What matters, of course, is what you want to do next. If you've been working in a not-for-profit organisation and want to move into the private sector, you will need to point to your successes. If you want to move into a sector where such language is seen as aggressively commercial, use a softer sub-heading like "key areas of experience".

ADDING A SUMMARY LIST OF SKILLS TO A "STRAIGHT-IN" CV

One important variation on the "straight-in" CV is where you add a *very short, very factual* summary of your skills. There is a simple test to see if this will help: does the information supplied on page 1 (mainly about your current role) say everything important? You might find that you also need to draw in skills and experience from deeper in your CV. If you find that this is a major problem, strongly consider the profile-led approach set out in Chapter 7. If it's just a question of bringing some pieces of information forward, try using a Skills Summary just after the contact details on your "straight-in" CV. The new format will look a little like this:

Format of page 1 of a "straight-in" CV with skills summary

Name

Address

Contact Details

Key skills

_____

Latest job

Overview of the role and organisation

_____

Key achievements: _____

_____

Previous job

Overview of the role and organisation

_____

Key achievements: _____

_____

1

An example of such a Skills Summary, which appeared on our business travel consultant's CV, is shown below.

Skills Summary

As a senior travel consultant I offer the following key skills and experience:

- *A track record of 12 years offering business travel solutions.*

- *Organising major international events.*

- *Highly developed planning, negotiation and customer service skills.*

- *Deep understanding of marketing from previous experience in the retail sector.*

- *Qualified member of the Chartered Institute of Marketing.*

The reason this CV needed this Skills Summary was (a) to emphasise the level of experience acquired by this candidate and (b) to bring out some key skills and qualifications that would otherwise have been hidden away on page 2.

COMPLETING YOUR "STRAIGHT-IN" CV

Once you have covered all the jobs you wish to discuss in detail, what remains is to wrap up the final pieces of information, namely:

1. Education and Qualifications

2. Training

3. Personal Information

4. Interests.

To incorporate this information and complete the remainder of your CV, turn to Chapter 10.

Front Page News: The Profile-led CV

This chapter helps you to:

▌ Look at the relative value of a profile-led CV

▌ Anticipate the impact of the first page of your CV

▌ Avoid classic page 1 errors

▌ See the opening page as a single-page advertisement

"You write to communicate to the hearts and minds of others what's burning inside you. And we edit to let the fire show through the smoke."

Arthur Polotnik

USING A PROFILE WHEN IT MATTERS

Why write a profile-led CV when recruiters say they don't like profiles? There are several reasons. One is that HR staff and line managers are far more open to profiles. The research doesn't say why, but do remember that there are different agendas here. A recruiter wants to present you to an employer in his or her own language, and they get irritated if you have already decided what your primary strengths are. An employer minds far less how you present your qualities, as long as there is a clear match to the job that needs filling.

You won't please everyone with it all the time (note particularly the section entitled **Using a profile-led CV with recruitment consultants** in Chapter 11). You will (inevitably) find someone who hates it. However, this is a model I have used repeatedly to help people get interviews and job offers in fields that they would otherwise have problems getting into.

The model does come with a health warning. If you include a profile (1) you **must** make it focused, free of flowery adjectives, linked to real evidence of achievement, in a language targeted at the right decision maker in the right organisation. And (2) your list of key experience and achievements needs to be equally focused, and, where possible, needs to show which organisation or job you were in when you used the skill. If you are unsure whether a profile-led CV will be right for you, turn back to Chapter 5. If you are persuaded that a "straight-in" CV might not suit your needs, read on.

The big problem for a lot of people writing CVs is that they want to move into a different kind of job – to get out of the sector they are in, to change occupations, to refresh their careers. This, in fact, describes a high proportion of the kind of people who seek careers advice. If you're relatively happy in your work and just looking for greater responsibility or a change of scenery, you don't have to do much rethinking. A "straight-in" CV is the best, no-nonsense solution.

But, if you really want to make a major change in your career, the chances are that you are going to find this at least a little bit difficult. Recruiters are all too eager to pigeon-hole you, and because employers read CVs very quickly they tend to exclude those who don't have immediately obvious experience. The emphasis must be on *tend to*. Sometimes skill shortages mean that employers have to look more widely. At other times a good CV may convince an employer that you do, in fact, have a lot to offer, even if you're CV isn't an exact match.

If you want to transform your career, changing role and, possibly, even sector as well, you have to do something more than communication. You have to *change the way others see you*, whether they are recruiters or employers. The profile-led CV is the only CV that is really capable of pulling this off. If you have to change the way someone thinks about you in a short space of time, you are going to have to pull this off on page 1.

The only page that matters?

Let's familiarise ourselves with the basic format of the profile-led CV.

Format for a profile-led CV

Name Address Contact Details **Profile** _____ _____ **Key Achievements** Theme 1: _____ _____ Theme 2: _____ _____ Theme 3: _____ _____ **Latest Job** Overview of the role and organisation _____ _____ Key achievements: _____ _____ _____ _____ _____ 1	**Previous Job** Overview of the role and organisation _____ _____ Key achievements: _____ _____ **Previous Job** Overview of the role and organisation _____ _____ Key achievements: _____ _____ **Qualifications** _____ _____ **Training Courses Attended** _____ _____ **Interests** _____ _____ 2

The great advantage of the profile-led CV is that it really majors on what happens on the first page. The intention is to steer the reader towards a particular conclusion by the time he or she has read the profile and key achievements section.

First page errors

You've already looked at CV problems in Chapter 3, but here is what typically goes wrong with the first page of a CV.

- **Upside down** – the CV starts with non-essential information, and hides the good stuff on page 2 or 3.

- **No clear message** – your CV fails to get its main points across.

- **Profile crash** – your initial summary confuses, irritates and sends out all the wrong messages or no message at all.

- **Over-egged** – your first page oversells you dreadfully (see Chapter 8 for examples).

- **Overload** – trying to make too many points at the same time.

- **Contradictory** – the reader gets two or three conflicting pictures.

- **Jumble sale** – it's full of disconnected information.

- **Wastes time on the obvious** – your CV offers no additional insights beyond what the general reader could guess from your list of job titles.

The top two-thirds rule

What happens when a reader looks at the first page? As it is true that most CVs are read at speed, the decision to call you for interview will be made very quickly. Imagine the first page of a CV. Imagine that a line is drawn across the page about a third up from the bottom. Look at the text that appears above the cut-off line. In all probability the reader will make some kind of decision by that point – a decision about whether you match the basic requirements of the job. This decision isn't about a job offer, but "should we get this person in for interview?".

The top two-thirds rule

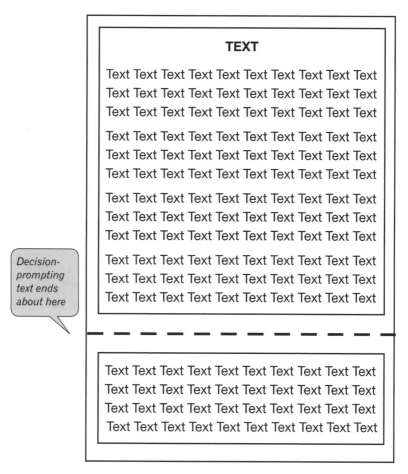

Just as busy readers only take in a proportion of information in any kind of published advertisement, the CV reader is always going to be selective. We have already looked at what puts a reader off. A busy CV reader will in my experience always be positively influenced by a relatively small number of factors: (a) bold text, (b) text that appears at the beginning of a line or a bullet point, (c) certain kind of content (e.g. job titles, names of organisations, specific named competencies) and (d) text that appears in the top two thirds of the first page of your document.

Look carefully at everything in the top 66% of page 1 of your profile-led CV. *Everything* there should be designed, as far as possible, to get you through the door. All of your key messages need to be on that first page, and most of the convincing evidence needs to be printed in the top 66% of page 1. Anything else on page 2 (and page 3 if you really need it) is simply supporting evidence that supports and reinforces *the decision the reader has already made*. The same is broadly true for a "straight-in" or functional CV – get the key messages across quickly or don't bother.

The first page of your CV should be a memorable A4 poster advertising *you*. That's the trick of page 1, and it's very simple. Unpack it from the top:

- Your first name is the same name you would use if answering the telephone.

- Your contact details are clear and up to date.

- Your profile is the right mix of **You/What/Next** (see Chapter 8).

- Your profile presents claims, supported by appropriately weighted adjectives, and links to evidence.

- You offer a relevant list of key experience, skills and achievements in bullet points that links very clearly to the top six or so competencies of the job.

- You provide evidence that your qualifications and training are sufficient.

- You give (if this is appropriate) a quick overview of your career.

HOW TO WRITE YOUR PROFILE-LED CV
Writing your CV backwards

As with the "straight-in" CV, it's easier to write page 2 of your CV first. This is even more true in the profile-led CV. It's virtually impossible to write a profile and list of achievements if you haven't trawled through a number of jobs. So, start with your work history first, tidy up the rest of page 2 and then move to page 1. For the sake of clarity the following sections are written in the order in which they will appear in your CV, not the order you will write them in.

Your contact details

Follow the guidelines given in Chapter 10.

The profile

The profile is obviously key. This is so important it gets its own chapter – Chapter 8.

Leave this part of your CV blank at this stage, and write it once you have finished the rest of page 1 *and* done most of the work on the body of your CV. In fact, you should always make the writing of the profile the very last job of writing your CV. If you try to write it straight away you will very probably get stuck or dispirited, and it will be difficult – largely because you haven't yet got a complete overview of your work history.

Key achievements and experience

Once you have learned how to set out relevant, punchy facts and evidence in the main body of your CV, where you work job-by-job through your recent work history, you should start to see certain themes and patterns emerging.

In the summary of "Key Achievements and Experience" on page 1 you set out a number of bullet points that capture the *relevant* highlights from your work history. In a profile-led CV this information comes before your work history, because you are getting the reader to look at all the key information about you in one place. These achievements don't necessarily have to come from your most recent job. However, if they don't, do try to make it clear which job you are relating to (for example, by mentioning a company name). Most items should ideally be taken from the last 2–3 years of your career (but go beyond this if you need to convey key information from further back or if you've been out of the labour market in recent years).

Don't attempt to write this section before you have recorded the highlights of each job you have undertaken before. Turn to Chapter 9 for detailed advice about how you capture your achievements on paper.

Qualifications and continuing professional development

It is optional whether this appears on page 1 of your CV or deeper inside it. The one and only guiding factor is *whether the information here is likely to get you shortlisted*. If your qualifications are not directly related to the role you're after, you may want to leave them until deeper in your CV. You may also want to do some explaining, some unpacking (what did you do in your studies that relates to your working life) and translating (what transferable skills did you acquire?). One of my clients was a sharp, business-focused accountant with a degree in Classics. He made play of the fact that his knowledge of the Roman Empire gave him a great grounding for the cut and thrust of organisational change.

Some organisations are looking for particular technical or professional qualifications (e.g. in Health and Safety or Accountancy or an MBA). If so, state that qualification loud and clear on page 1. Employers no longer expect you to put the date of a qualification on your CV, but you should say where and how you studied for the qualification, and (if appropriate) what grade or standard you achieved. If you undertook a special project, or a particular area of research, consider including this if you can make it relevant to your reader.

Job-by-job details

Use the job-by-job approach outlined in Chapter 6, pulling out achievements against each role. Some of these achievements will be transferred to the summary list on page 1. You may find the **Role Analysis Sheet** in Chapter 6 useful to help you draw out relevant evidence from each job.

Completing your "profile-led" CV

Once you have covered all the jobs you wish to discuss in detail, what remains is to wrap up the final pieces of information, namely training, personal information and interests. Chapter 10 will show you how to complete these elements in your CV.

A REFINEMENT – THE ONE-PAGE AD MODEL

The variation of the profile-led CV proposed in this chapter is the one-page ad model. In outline form it looks like this.

Format of the "one-page ad" CV model

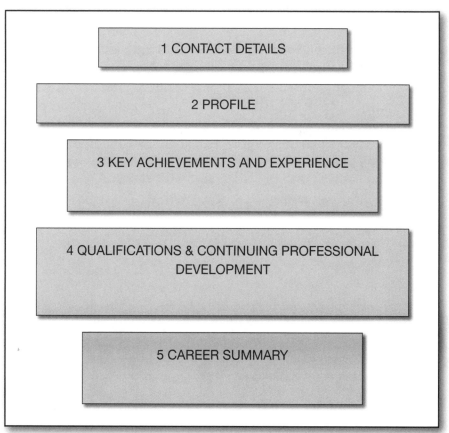

1 CONTACT DETAILS

2 PROFILE

3 KEY ACHIEVEMENTS AND EXPERIENCE

4 QUALIFICATIONS & CONTINUING PROFESSIONAL DEVELOPMENT

5 CAREER SUMMARY

The layout of the first page should be sharp, clear, with plenty of white space. Think of it as a number of blocks of information (although, please note that it's best not to use boxes or lines as special effects). Note that the blocks of text vary in terms of widths and length, and are laid with plenty of space in between.

What makes the one-page ad model different? It takes the profile-led CV one step further by getting all the key information onto one page:

- An overview of who you are, what you have to offer.

- A summary of your key skills (or, if required, competencies) and achievements.

- Reference to key qualifications, training or continuing professional development.

- An at-a-glance picture of your CV as a whole.

What the one-page ad model adds to the basic profile-led CV is (a) some reference to qualifications on page 1 and, more significantly, (b) a career summary – discussed at the end of this chapter. Let's use an example of a real CV to demonstrate a fairly good profile-led model that adopted the one-page ad model in order to change sectors. As with our "straight-in" CV example, this CV has been abbreviated to fit on the page:

There's no need to title your document "Curriculum Vitae", which looks very old-fashioned. Print your name as you wish it to be used at interview

Clear contact details including an email address

ALISON RICHARDS

16 Durham Close
Newtown, Shropshire
SY16 2MN
Tel: 01691 876543   Email: ar1@example.com

Keywords on the top line or towards the left-hand side of text

*The **profile** is a short paragraph of no more than four sentences saying what sort of role you have in mind, your current role or position, your key experience to date and what you can offer an employer*

PROFILE

An experienced communications professional with a background in HR and people development, with a strong track record of designing and implementing in-house communication solutions in the pharmaceutical, food and IT sectors. A clear-thinking graduate with well-developed powers of persuasion in speech and writing. Seeking a role that builds on proven change management, motivation and team-building skills.

KEY ACHIEVEMENTS AND EXPERIENCE

*List your **achievements** briefly, using bullet points, and offering examples that you think will be most relevant to a future employer in your chosen field*

- Designing, co-ordinating and delivering a comprehensive communication programme across all group companies during a merger transition period

- Managing a team to re-design and deliver a 'new-look' group website

- Designing and managing the roll-out of a new corporate identity programme across all companies and locations

- Establishing and managing production of a Global Company Magazine for staff

- Selling the Intranet communications to the board of directors

- Designing and conducting a UK-wide staff training programme

- Establishing a group-wide Intranet and communications policy

- National Student of the Year for CIM exams.

QUALIFICATIONS/CONTINUING PROFESSIONAL DEVELOPMENT

If space allows separate each section clearly

History BA (Hons.) 2.1, Manchester University

CIPD Qualification, Farnborough College

A Levels in History (A), English (B), Economics (C)

Key qualifications and training courses, with grades. Again, lead with the topic rather than the data or institution

RECENT CAREER SUMMARY

Nicetech Pharmaceuticals	Communications Manager	2001–2007
Chocolate UK	Internal Communications Manager	1998–2001
Giant Telcoms	HR and Communications Manager	1992–1998
Giant Telcoms	HR Assistant	1986–1992

Your career ladder – at a glance. Lead with either the company name or your job title – whichever has most impact

Lead with job title on left, followed by organisation name, location and years employed

DETAILED CAREER HISTORY

Begin your job-by-job history on page 1 or 2, depending on space

Communications Manager, Nicetech   (2001 to date)
Responsible for setting and rolling out policy regarding internal communications, and for managing an in-house communication team

- Designed, co-ordinated and delivered a comprehensive internal communication programme across all European locations, with particular emphasis within the UK

- Introduced a European Newsletter – sourced business, technical and human-interest stories from nine European sites, organized translation services

- Initiated, designed and implemented a new group-wide company Intranet

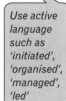

Use active language such as 'initiated', 'organised', 'managed', 'led'

Internal Communications Manager – Chocolate UK (1998–2001)
Responsible for all aspects of internal communications, and for launching and editing an in-house magazine

- Initiated a communications programme reaching out to 13,500 staff across Europe

- Organized and managed a very successful Royal Visit to open our new site

- Produced a 'diary-style' video of the preparations for, and the actual Royal Visit

- Organized Groundbreaking ceremony and Public Relations activities for a multi-company training initiative

- Member of the Site Executive Management Team responsible for managing an HR team, providing a comprehensive generalist HR service supporting 300 people

- Introduced our site-wide Team Briefing process – ran training sessions for managers

Use high-energy language in your bullet points

Hr & Comms Manager, Giant Telecoms (1992–1998)

Initially an HR role, this was expanded in 1996 to include a responsibility for all HR activities including: communications, recruitment, remuneration, 'downsizing', employee relations, performance management, training and development

- Launched a management development programme leading to Investors in People (IIP) status

- Researched, designed and implemented a 'shop floor to top floor' pay and grading system

- Designed and introduced a competency-based appraisal and recruitment programme

TRAINING COURSES ATTENDED

- **Web page design** using FrontPage

- **Ability Testing and Personality Profiling** (SHL)

- **Handling the Media**

- **Facilitator Training**

- **Presentation Skills**

- **Management Skills Programme** (ABC)

- **Software proficiency:** Microsoft Word, PowerPoint, Excel, Outlook, Project, FrontPage 2000, Photoshop CS

Mention training (including courses that did not lead to a certificate) as well as qualifications. Lead with the main focus of the training event on the left-hand side

INTERESTS

Hill walking, kayaking, trustee of local disability charity and improving my spoken Italian.

Mention languages

Include interests that might be relevant to the job, those that indicate co-operative or team working, or simply things you can talk about at interview with enthusiasm

The (very optional) Career Summary

The example CV above uses a Career Summary, something you don't always see on a CV. It can add enormous clarity – or it can completely mess things up. So it needs using with care, and only if it's useful.

The idea of the Career Summary is that it presents your entire work history at a glance, starting with your most recent job. Career summaries can be useful if you have worked in a variety of well-known organisations and you want to get this point across quickly. If you have been working for more than 15–20 years you may not need to include earlier jobs in your Career Summary. A summary will also be useful if you want to demonstrate that you have experience of a range of sectors.

The major disadvantage of a Career Summary is that it prevents you from including detailed information about your most recent job on page 1 of your CV. It also makes it more likely that you will run to three pages rather than two. It is probably best avoided if you have worked for one organisation for a long time and do not wish to ram that piece of information down a recruiter's throat. And, finally, as if these facts aren't enough to put you off, it is disliked by recruitment consultants.

So why consider it at all? There are times when the only thing that is going to get you into an interview is a good one-page ad CV, and sometimes a Career Summary adds an extra element of clarity. The key question is: does it help with the overall message of page 1? If it doesn't, have no hesitation leaving it out.

When you might use a career summary in your CV:

- When you want to do something quite different to your last job.

- When you want to change sector or role, or both.

- When you want to draw attention to previous roles on the first page of your CV.

- When you can show a clear history of progression and promotion.

- When you can list several well-known organisations.

- When it is helpful to show experience in a range of roles or sectors.

- When you have achieved above-average progression.

- When you have made career changes and want to show at a glance how your career "fits together".

When you should probably NOT to use a career summary in your CV:

- When you have been with the same organisation for a long time (although it is still worth considering if you have undertaken a wide range of roles, so you are demonstrating that you have enjoyed a career inside one organisation).

- When you have problem gaps in your CV.

- Where you have changed jobs very frequently.

- When you have worked for a number of small or obscure employers who will not be known to the recruiter.

- Where your career summary does not suggest any kind of structure or pattern and looks like an unconnected series of roles.

- Where you have limited work experience.

The Exact Art of Profile Writing

This chapter helps you to:

I Learn the value of a well-constructed CV profile

I Avoid the classic errors and pitfalls of profile writing

I Understand the key elements in a good profile

I Apply the "so what?" test

I Link your profile to your personal branding statement

"It requires a very unusual mind to undertake the analysis of the obvious."

Alfred N Whitehead

SINK OR SWIM – THE CV PROFILE

If you have decided to use a profile, you'll quickly discover it's the most difficult thing to compose, but probably the most useful thing you will write – even if you don't use it.

Why wouldn't you use it? Some recruiters don't like CVs with profiles in, and some candidates prefer not to use them. Fine – CV writing is an art, not a science. Whether you use a profile or not, it's a good idea to write one. It gets you really focused on the key issues around your job search. In fact, your CV profile is fairly close to the kind of verbal summary of yourself you might find useful in a networking or social context – see **Your Personal Branding Statement** at the end of this chapter.

You will see some CV guides telling you that the profile has had its day. As someone who regularly assists people into the top end of the market- place, I can assure you that it hasn't. What will no longer fly is the over- written, shallow profile that is overstuffed with empty adjectives. Use punchy, concrete and focused language. In our CV survey, one respond- ent approved of the "greater effective use of achievement summaries at the beginning of CVs". Profiles are only welcome if they are strongly connected to the job and give clear reasons why you should be invited to interview.

Our CV survey appears to show that well-written profiles are acceptable to employers. One HR manager praised "better attempts to tailor really key information into the earlier part of the CV; genuine attempts to demonstrate 'fit' to the requirements". "The 'potted' summary", accord- ing to one HR director, "is always a good indication of if you should read any further". Another felt that CVs "seem to be becoming more 'user friendly', with most important data on first page".

In our survey one HR specialist sent in a sample of the kind of profile she hates: "I am a confident, hard-working and self-motivated indi- vidual who is used to people-facing roles and can communicate and liaise with people both within and without all levels of an organisation. I have a friendly and approachable manner and possess excellent com- munication skills, which I believe makes me a real team player". A busy recruiter is deeply unimpressed by this kind of profile, and will skim- read it with little enthusiasm. Like it or not, most recruiters pigeonhole people into five categories: "strong fit", "reasonable fit", "uncertain fit", "not a fit" or "don't know". Unless your CV gets you into one of the first two categories in the first sift, you're going nowhere.

TIGHTENING UP YOUR PROFILE

Here's an example of one candidate's CV profile at a rough first draft stage.

Example Profile 1 – Logistics Supervisor (Initial Draft)
Richard L. Davies

I am a committed and loyal staff member with an excellent attendance record. I have worked my way up from entry positions in a range of occupations, and gained important experience in distribution and logistics. I am now returning to the labour market after retraining. I am looking for an opportunity to prove myself as a hard-working and highly motivated team player who will add value to your business.

Recruiters see a lot of CVs that begin like this. The problem with writing a profile in the first person is that it can sound like a begging letter. Writing "I am" three times is repetitive. The profile is stuffed full of phrases that sound positive but are not linked to examples or evidence. More worrying, the profile draws attention to things that an employer almost takes for granted, e.g. "excellent attendance record" and "hard working". It's almost as if this candidate wants to be thanked for doing the ordinary, basic parts of the job.

One sentence at a time

A profile needs to be concise to be effective. Therefore it's unlikely to be more than four or five sentences long. Let's agree on four – if you can't get the message across in four sentences, it's probably too complicated. There are no absolute rules for how those should flow, but "You/What/Next" is a good structure to begin with:

CV Profile Writing: You/What/Next

a) **You:** Who you are in terms of occupational background, experience and sector knowledge.

b) **What:** What do you have to offer in terms of know-how and skills, what have you done and achieved? **What else?** What in your mix of skills and experience makes you unusual or attractive?

c) **Next:** What's next? What kind of role, organisation, culture and challenges would provide the right next step for you?

Sentence 1 – *you*

Look again at the first sentence of the profile for Richard Davies: "I am a committed and loyal staff member with an excellent attendance record". It is the first full sentence of the CV, and is therefore the sentence read with greatest attention. It is the paper equivalent of your first 30 seconds in the job interview: first impressions count.

Whether your CV is read by someone junior to the final decision maker, or by a busy manager, it's vital to get the **you** message in your profile absolutely right. Most CVs attempt the problem of saying who you are by coming up with similar empty phrases. The problem with terms like "committed", "loyal" and "energised" is that they are difficult to prove on paper. Worse still, they are undifferentiated messages – everyone out there presents themselves as "highly motivated", as a "team player", a "great communicator" and so on.

Make every word count in that vital first sentence. Try to summarise your occupational role. When describing **you**, find the right mix of sector and job title, even if it's not an exact job title taken from your CV. For example, "qualified laboratory supervisor with extensive experience in the pharmaceutical sector" is clear, focused, and a good indication of role, responsibility and sector experience.

Link this information to clues about your academic background and professional status. Using the word "graduate" in your profile (e.g. "graduate sales manager with 10 years' experience in the automotive sector") probably says as much as you want to say. A professional qualification or MBA can also be mentioned quickly and economically (e.g. "MBA-qualified communications office manager").

After some work Richard's opening sentence was rewritten as follows.

> *An MBA-qualified professional with 12 years' successful track record in distribution, transport and warehouse organisation.*

This first sentence is brief, but gets across several key messages (qualification, track record, sectoral background, seniority).

Sentences 2 & 3 – *what?/what else?*

Richard's original profile contained the following second and third sentences: "*I have worked my way up from entry positions in a range of occupations, and gained important experience in distribution and logistics. I am now returning to the labour market after retraining*". These two sentences avoid making claims, apart from the rather weak "important experience". However, they don't really work, and introduce some potentially negative thoughts in the mind of the recruiter – a range of occupations? Is this a person who finds it difficult to stick to one career path? Why did he need to leave the labour market and get retrained?

Sentences 2 and 3 are the **what** message: they capture what you have done in a nutshell. Your CV is going to spend a lot more time discussing your experience and achievements, but these are the main headlines behind your story.

If you have worked in a variety of sectors *and* you think that will help, you might want to use that information here. Your main focus, however, should be on creating a message that shouts out "achievement" rather than potential. If you're relatively new to the labour market (which will include those who have taken time out for other purposes) don't let this put you off. Even if you have relatively little recent work experience you should be able to say something about past results (in short-term, temporary jobs or work placements, or in voluntary work, or in your outside interests, or in your studies – probably in that order of priority).

To write sentence 2 you need to take an overview of your career, *looked at from the perspective of your most recent successes*. So a sentence that begins "*Starting with a degree in Business Studies, and after setting up my own business as a freelance photographer, I have most recently become an HR specialist*" fails, by offering the reader far too many distractions along the way. A better, simpler approach might read: "*A graduate HR professional with extensive experience of recruitment and training, built on previous experience and study of the business world*".

Here is the rewritten **what** section from Richard's new profile:

> *A highly experienced manager with experience of cutting-edge IT systems, supported by a background in supervisory roles in the logistics, catering and printing sectors.*

Now the emphasis is indeed on recent success, and manages once again to get across several complementary pieces of information – industry background, current role and status, and one factor that will help to distinguish him from the competition.

Final Sentence – *next*

In two sentences (it might take three, but no more) you've established who you are and what you have done. The last sentence is about what, ideally, is your **next** step – where you want to be and what you bring to the party.

Richard's present offering is this: "*I am looking for an opportunity to prove myself as a hard-working and highly motivated team player who will add value to your business*". This just doesn't cut the mustard. First, it's straying into empty claims that do more damage than good. Writing in a CV that you're "hard working" makes a recruiter worry that perhaps you're the opposite but trying to dig yourself out of a hole. It is, however, a good idea to make some kind of a link between **what** and **next**. The best way to this is often to point to a skill that makes you distinctive, and write about your interest in exercising this in a new context. This works well because it demonstrates a clear motivation for job change.

The other opportunity you have in your **next** sentence is to write about the next step you might like to take. Some career coaches and recruiters recommend that you name a specific target job, e.g.: "*currently seeking a role as a Marketing Director in the fmcg sector*". If you really have just one job in your sights, this might work. The problem is that your target job has to be *stated in words that are meaningful to each and every potential employer*. You might use a target job statement with a recruitment consultant, but they are virtually useless in CVs sent directly to employers. Putting in the title of the job you're applying for looks artificial and pushy. Equally, including a target job that is a poor match for the role on offer means you're sunk. In CVs to employers it's a better idea to make your statement more general, for example Richard's revised **next** statement in his profile:

> *Currently seeking a decision-making role in a forward-looking logistics organisation with a passion for motivating staff towards continual performance improvement.*

Combined effect – the completed profile

Finally, as Richard is known as Rick to everyone he has ever worked with, that's how he will title his CV. Here's the revised profile as a whole:

> **Rick Davies**
>
> *An MBA-qualified professional with 12 years' successful track record in distribution, transport and warehouse organisation. A highly experienced manager with experience of cutting-edge IT systems, supported by a background in supervisory roles in the logistics, catering and printing sectors. Currently seeking a decision-making role in a forward-looking logistics organisation with a passion for motivating staff towards continual performance improvement.*

Notice that the new profile includes a more focused mix of *claims* and *evidence*, and now includes a defined (but not too prescriptive) target job and organisation. It is now in the third person, attempting to avoid saying "he is" or "Rick is" but beginning each sentence with the kind of CV shorthand ("A highly experienced user ...") is perfectly acceptable in today's marketplace – it might not win any essay prizes, but compared to most garbled email and text English it's very clear. In our survey one HR manager complained about the use of the third person in CVs, although this was only one response out of many.

Different examples of profiles are set out below, along with comments about why they might succeed or fail. We begin by looking at two "overcooked" profiles.

> **Example Profile 2**
>
> *An overcooked profile for a business analyst*
>
> *A successful, experienced and focused IT business analyst with a background in financial applications within an SAP environment. Talented at managing teams, with well-developed negotiation skills and recent exposure to a large-scale company integration. A professional, results-oriented graduate with an excellent academic record and a track record of success, well respected by colleagues and managers alike. A hard-working and committed individual who strives to deliver a quality result for the business and its customers.*

This is half way there, but has too many adjectives per line. The 74 words in the profile include the following adjectival phrases: *successful/experienced/focused/talented with well-developed negotiation skills/ professional/results-oriented/graduate/with an excellent academic record/track record of success/well respected/hard working/committed/ strives to deliver*. All high-blown claims, with barely a single piece of evidence in sight.

The problem with an overcooked profile is that you have lost an opportunity to make a strong first impression and pushed the reader into a hostile position. Our survey confirms the fact that employers dislike "people overselling themselves in their CVs". Another respondent complained about the mismatch between profile and reality: "Personally, I do not like the personal profile paragraph unless it says something specific. Naturally, only positives are going to be highlighted, but too many profiles say that the individual is a good communicator, etc., but this is often not backed up at interview". A reworked version of the IT Business Analyst profile might read as follows:

> **Redrafted profile for an IT business analyst**
>
> *A highly experienced graduate business analyst with good working knowledge of a range of financial applications and a track record of success in SAP environments. Well-developed leadership, negotiation and change management skills. Now seeking a challenging role in an organisation determined to achieve quality results and the highest levels of customer satisfaction.*

Now to an overcooked graduate profile.

> **Example Profile 3**
>
> *An overcooked profile for a recent graduate*
>
> *A creative, clear thinking graduate with wide-ranging experience gained in a number of media-related temporary positions. An experienced communicator with excellent written and verbal skills and wide-ranging experience of working in many different environments. I am focused and determined, and have excellent powers of persuasion. My previous posts have required me to be flexible, to use my own initiative, work well in a team, have a sense of humour and to be able to prioritise workloads. I am very well organised in my methods of working and enjoy paying attention to detail.*

In all fairness, it's tough writing a profile if you're a graduate new to the marketplace, especially when you don't have much in the way of work experience to draw upon. This is a very typical offering. It translates as "I have very little experience, but great potential". The first sentence feels like an apology – "I haven't had a proper job in the media". This profile also makes the mistake of thinking that a CV is like playing the roulette table – place bets on as many numbers as possible and something must come up. The problem is that the profile tends to write about qualities rather than skills.

This candidate's career coach got back to basics: "what have you actually done (in your studies, in your temporary work, on work experience, anywhere … ?)". The revised version is set out below:

> **Redrafted recent graduate profile**
>
> *A clear-thinking graduate with experience in the leisure management, communication and PR sectors. Proven written communications skills, excellent powers of persuasion and public speaking ability (to business as well as student audiences), accompanied by a track record of getting teams to achieve results on time and on target. Now seeking a role in broadcasting or communication that draws on the ability to anticipate audience demands and deliver effective communication solutions.*

Swiftly followed by a list of key experience and achievements that offers linked examples of all the above.

Example Profile 4

Computing graduate

Highly experienced computing graduate working as IS Development Manager with skills across broad ranges of hardware and software systems. Experienced in IBM AS/400, IBM System 34/36/38, MS Project, RPG III & IV. Skilled within international, multi-site, multi-company structures. Uniquely combines an eye for detail with a flair for developing creative solutions, to facilitate the co-ordination of important, complex and high-value projects.

This profile is a good example of the power (or limiting effect) of the opening four or five words. If you tell the reader that you're a computing graduate in a computing job, you can't really be surprised if, like this candidate, you're not invited for project management or general management roles. For a purely technical job this profile might work, but it's clear from the final sentence that this candidate wants to break out of the box and move into a more general project management role. If so, the jargon is off-putting. A better profile would translate IT experience into the language of business solutions, and bring out more transferable skills.

Redrafted computing graduate profile

Highly experienced graduate systems development manager with broad experience of international, multi-site and multi-company structures. Strong technical background is combined with effective people skills and a flair for developing creative solutions. Seeking a role managing creative projects from concept to implementation.

Next, a style of profile writing that sets off all kinds of alarm bells – the "flowery adjectives" profile.

Example Profile 5

The opening of a "flowery adjectives" profile

A talented, dynamic performer, I am a good communicator in speech and writing, with a mix of analytical and creative thinking. Highly motivated and a strong team player, I am seeking the next big challenge ... .

The flowery adjectives profile sets off all kinds of alarm bells for an employer. Are you going to come out with this kind of nonsense when talking about the organisation? This approach makes huge claims, but where's the evidence? Also there is a very strong sense that this candidate is trying to be all things to all people. Even if you get to interview stage, you're wearing a big round target sticker. The interviewer is going to have a field day probing the facts (or lack of them) and demolishing your claims so fast that the only thing on your CV you're prepared to defend is your name and address.

Here are three examples of fairly effective profiles:

Example Profile 6

European sales manager

Dynamic, French native, multi-lingual European Sales Manager with excellent influencing skills plus 7 years' experience in successfully building and leading sales operations for major European corporations. Demonstrable results in working across varying cultures, building key accounts, and making a significant contribution to organisational efficiency, growth and profitability. Seeking a challenging opportunity to develop sales management of high-quality, luxury brands across European markets.

This is a reasonably well-constructed profile. Simple, straightforward, fairly free of floating adjectives and extremely easy to see that this one fits the "You/What/Next" structure – it's clear what this candidate has done, when and where she is going.

Now to a profile which attempts to get a complex job across in a way that will appeal to a particular kind of corporate target reader, and at the same time argues a case for transferable skills.

Example Profile 7

Retail manager

An MBA-qualified information and records specialist with a background in scientific, technical and environmental issues. Fully familiar with the range of IT solutions available, and with a track record of analysing, organising and implementing effective information solutions. Strong awareness of general company law, structure of companies and wider legal implications of operating businesses, such as data protection, safety, environmental and labour law.

Example Profile 8

A direct, simple profile written in the first person

I have a thorough retail understanding at an operational and strategic level gained from a successful track record with leading brands such as Marks & Spencer and the Burton Group, including international and business development experience. I am motivated by adding value. I have the respect of my peers and my approach is based upon confident leadership, passion, fun and sound personal ethics. Amongst many other things, my love for travel has given me a healthy perspective on the importance of cultural awareness in the personal and professional arena.

Only few candidates, with strong and very clear track records, can risk using words like "thorough" and "strategic". This profile is well matched to a work history with two recent roles at senior level in the retail sector.

The "so what?" test

Too many of the draft profiles presented in this chapter fail the easiest, most important, test you can apply to a draft CV – the "**so what?**" **test**. Line by line, read your CV and ask "so what?" after each phrase. Wherever you mention a responsibility, a skill, an achievement, the same question: "so what?". In CVs for relatively senior people I often find phrases like "Responsible for staff training" or "Responsible for recruitment and selection" or "Undertook annual appraisals of staff".

So what? Any candidate with a history of formal management will have done these things. Mentioning them makes the document sound like a CV for a far less experienced person. Equally, a phrase like "IT competent" may fail the same test – better to point to a real familiarity with computer applications. If you find anything in your CV that would be true of virtually all candidates, either sharpen it or cut it out. The exception would be experience or qualifications which will keep you off the shortlist if you don't mention them. Equally, consider chopping out empty adjectives such as "hard working", "committed" and "motivated" – unless you have above-average achievement examples to back them up.

Making your pitch

As you will no doubt have guessed, the way a good CV profile works is very similar to "pitching" an idea to a busy decision maker. A recruiter will typically forward four or five CVs to a busy employer and will spend no more than about 3–4 minutes explaining why each candidate should be seen. In the business world people pitch products and services to busy buyers. You will from time to time be required to pitch a new idea at a busy executive. A director pitches an idea for a new movie to a studio executive. Authors pitch new book titles. Politicians try to condense policy in memorable sound bites. We all pitch. Your CV, backed up by your interview performance, does pretty much the same thing, except in today's world of information overload you have seconds, not minutes, to get the right decision.

Your personal branding statement

Your message is contained in everything you send out (letters, CV, emails), and everything you say. It's what you say when someone asks you at a party "what kind of thing are you looking for?". You might answer with a long, sad story about the difficulties of your job search. Don't. It wins sympathy, but rarely leads to a recommendation. You might use a job title, saying something like "I'm looking for work as a project manager". Fine, but even networking contacts rarely have vacancies up their sleeve.

What works best is a short summary, not much longer than your CV profile, of who you are, your *motivated skills* (the skills you perform at the highest level and enjoy using) and the kind of organisation you'd like to work for. It's a verbal match to your CV profile. You might also talk about the style (high-tech, customer-focused …) and culture of the organisation (private, public, blue-chip, privately owned …).

Employers, recruitment consultants and networking contacts can respond well to that this kind of pitch when it is clear, succinct, memorable and packed with enthusiasm. What's more, people respond in a completely different way compared to simply asking about job opportunities. When they hear your message, listeners hear a set of ingredients and start to put them together into a meal. They say things like "You know, you really should talk to my friend Rashid …" or "Have you thought about talking to Acme Industries …" or, best of all, "That sounds to me like …" – when they identify a sector or field you haven't yet fallen across.

I encourage all my clients to work hard on composing a short verbal personal branding statement that sums up who you are and where you want to get to. You'll also hear it described as the "Elevator Pitch" – what you would say to an interviewer who meets you in reception and, travelling up in the lift, asks you to answer the question "tell me about yourself" between floors.

Broadcasting Your Achievements

This chapter helps you to:

I List your key achievements in a credible and focused way

I Support claims with evidence

I Edit your history down into effective bullet points

I Record and analyse your skills

I Use the Skills Triangle

"You can only become truly accomplished at something you love. Don't make money your goal. Instead, pursue the things you love doing, and then do them so well that people can't take their eyes off you."

Maya Angelou

BEEFING UP THE EVIDENCE

You have now decided on the kind of CV you will use, and got a structure and some data down on paper. The following chapter is useful no matter which format of CV you use. It focuses on how you communicate evidence.

An effective CV contains not just claims about what you can do, but solid evidence, and the best kind of evidence of your skills and know-how is contained in defined achievements. It's very common for people to be poor at spotting their own achievements. In our British culture we tend to criticise more than affirm. However, an awful lot of people fail to communicate their strengths either in a CV or at interview, which serves no-one's interest, no matter how modest.

MODESTY

Career coaches spend so much time telling their clients to "blow your own trumpet" you'd think they were frustrated brass players. It's important for us to recognise that many of us find writing about "achievements" very difficult. The British culture still (thankfully) cultivates an appropriate sense of modesty. However, while believing you're the best is usually a happy state of self-deception, understanding what makes you distinctive is a healthy step. Overdone modesty just doesn't work in a CV. In the usual 30-second dash through your CV a busy recruiter just doesn't have the time to unpack your language, to put two and two together, and to draw the right conclusion. If your CV says that you were "involved in restructuring the accounts department" it sounds like you were only involved in a background capacity. If you meant that you initiated and pushed through the most radical changes in your department for a decade, then say so.

One of the reasons some CV writers choose excessive modesty as a writing strategy is past experience of being savaged by an interviewer. It's all too easy for a recruiter to pull you to pieces if your CV makes outrageous or false claims. More often than not it's too easy to spot the empty claims from people who claim to be self-starters, achievers and team players – there is often no evidence at all to back up these assertions.

In fact, many claims you make about personality traits in a CV bounce badly as far as the reader is concerned. "Someone blowing their trumpet too loudly, particularly about their personality, rather than their achievements" was a bête noire for one HR manager. You are on much safer ground talking about your skills, because these are real – you possess them, and you can prove it with evidence from your past.

Let's refresh ourselves with the facts: what are employers really looking for? Snapshot responses from our survey included: "Hard facts – basic details number of people, turnover, change in profitability, etc." ... "Evidence of progression through an organisation or between organisations" ... "80% match to advert".

SKILLS RECORD

To begin to find the evidence you need, start by cataloguing your key skills as follows:

1. Divide a piece of A4 paper into three columns, as shown below in the **Skills Record**.

2. Go through your work history. You might do this by going through an old CV with a highlighter pen. Pull out all the important events, activities, situations and problems.

3. Use each item as a new line – briefly record the context, what happened in terms of activity and what you did (naming the skills you used).

Skills Record

CONTEXT	ACTIVITY	SKILLS
Document scanning project	*Training three temp staff*	*Planning* *Communication* *Leadership* *Supervision* *Organising workloads*

If you haven't time to go through every stage of your work history and you want to go straight to your key achievements, use the Skills Record above as a prompt. For a more detailed job-by-job approach, use the **Role Analysis Sheet** in Chapter 6. For the more developed analysis required when you look at competencies, see the **7 Step Competency Flow Chart** in Chapter 12.

SKILLS TRIANGLE

Another tool you might use is the Skills Triangle (see below). This is familiar to readers of my book *Take Control of Your Career*, and also useful here. The tool is designed to help people to communicate their skills to employers by learning to use a simple story structure.

The Skills Triangle

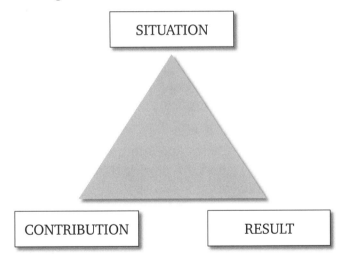

Begin with a **situation** – a context, i.e. a time and place where you used the particular skill. It doesn't have to be an earth-shattering event. Even the small stuff picks up your skill set. Next, think about your individual **contribution**. What did you do? If your contribution was part of a team, what was your team role and how effectively did you fulfil it? Finally, don't forget to record the final outcome – the **result**. Think about what key decision makers (here or in another company) consider to be worthwhile outcomes.

WRITING OUT YOUR ACHIEVEMENTS

Sadly, too many people fail to recognise their own skills, and even when the skills are identified they refuse to see them as anything out of the ordinary – *that's what everyone does.* Those who are sensitive to their impact on others find it almost physically painful to come out with simple, assertive statements of their strengths. Here are some tips that will help:

- Start with the facts; look at your actual achievements.

- Write down the language that an extrovert boss in your organisation would use in describing what you have done.

- Imagine you are writing the description about someone else you admire and want to help.

- Enlist the help of someone creative to come up with better ways of describing what you have done.

- Recruit the help of someone more assertive than you to come up with stronger ways of selling what you have done.

- Interrogate your writing for signs of excessive "spin". Would your claim stand up to probing questions?

Even though you have a little more leeway here than you do in the profile of your CV, it's important to keep to a strictly economical use of language. Learn how to keep things brief, focused and make each bullet point count.

Having thought about your achievements using one of the above approaches, you may start by writing down something rather lengthy like this:

Achievement Draft 1

- *Having looked at all in-house communication, I had the idea of launching an in-company newsletter. I took the idea to my boss, took responsibility to design a cover, and wrote the text for a pilot issue. I had to run the idea past the MD to get permission to print off copies for all UK locations, so the newsletter went out to 644 people. I redesigned the newsletter 2 years later, first of all as an attachment sent out by email, later we organised an interactive email that allowed users to click through to interesting pages.*

Everything you read here is interesting. In fact, this is about the right length for a good interview answer. But it's too long for a CV – readers often don't want to take the time to go through blocks of text. Secondly it uses phrases that sound **repetitive** ("I had the idea" … , "I had to run the idea …").

The next problem is that it takes **too many words** to make each point. The long opening sentence *"Having looked at all in-house communication, I had the idea of launching an in-company newsletter"* runs the risk of losing the reader. The last sentence is even longer, and complicated by sub-clauses. The text lacks bite. In our CV survey employers repeatedly asked for clear language that gets to the point. To get your point across effectively you need to use active language. First, avoid the passive voice. Don't write "A plan was established", write "I planned". Don't write "This activity led to receipt of a design award", write "The team won a design award". Wherever possible, **claim the things you did personally**. "I organised" is fine. "We organised" is weaker – what was the extent of your participation?

Nearly every sentence in the above draft paragraph begins with "I". If you decide to use the first person in your CV (see below regarding use of the third person), avoid over-repetition of "I" at the beginning of every bullet point and paragraph. The first decision regarding page 1 of your CV is whether you use the first person ("I led") or the third person ("he led"). Some readers in our survey say they find it odd to see "he achieved" or "she led" in a CV, although only a minority stated that this was a problem. Equally, many career changers find it odd to write a CV as if they were describing somebody else.

Finally, we want to get all the information in this paragraph down to a single bullet point, ideally one that will be only one or two lines long. Two full lines in a bullet point looks like continuous text, which the reader may ignore, so try to complete some sentences before you reach the right-hand side of the page.

How do you abbreviate it? Ask the question **what's the main point here?** In this case it's to show initiative, drive and demonstrate a skill. So our revised bullet point looks like this:

Achievement Final Draft

Negotiated and launched UK-wide company newsletter (readership 600+). Designed and wrote all material in text and web-based versions

---

You might have noticed that the above bullet point sounds and feels rather different. This rewrite draws on an alternative to saying "I", "he" or "she" by using what you might describe as the **'smart' third person**. It usually allows you to cut one word per sentence and, more importantly, it means that each achievement bullet point starts with a verb or a skill, e.g.:

Key Achievements and Experience

- *Organised ...*

- *Led ...*

- *Developed ...*

- *Managed ...*

- *Initiated ...*

- *Secured ...*

- *Trained ...*

While doing this you will quickly discover the importance of **active language** – verbs that are short, punchy, and carry a sense of energy and commitment. See the table below for a list of examples.

Active Verbs	
Less active	*More Active*
Put together	Shaped
Contributed to the planning of	Planned
Discussed	Communicated
Administered	Organised
Supervised	Managed
Encouraged	Motivated

Organised	Led
Started	Initiated
Brought on board	Convinced
Started	Launched
Compiled	Wrote
Trained	Coached
Re-organised	Refreshed
Became involved with	Committed to
Began with difficulty	Kick-started
Took through	Steered
Discussed with	Persuaded
Agreed	Negotiated
Concluded	Achieved
Communicated the benefits	Sold
Helped to grow	Expanded
Responded well to problems	Solution-focused
Attention to detail	Quality control
Co-operative	Flexible
Completed project	Achieved target

Having looked at this list, use words and phrases that feel **authentically right for you**. Too often candidates use longer, more official-sounding words (e.g. "utilised", "vacated", "corresponded with") when shorter words work better (e.g. "used", "left", "wrote to"). "Cut" is better than "abbreviated", "grew" better than "maximised".

Brief, everyday language works best in slogans ("no individual was ever terminated for purchasing an IBM computer" doesn't get you to the point like the less elegant "nobody ever got fired for …". Most of the time the same is true for CVs. In the end, the language has to work for you *and* for the reader.

OFFER CONCRETE EVIDENCE

Here's an example set of achievements taken from a functional CV.

Business Development

Developed a new set of clients in a previously unexplored industry sector and created business opportunities for my company

Client Servicing

Maintained customer accounts and provided professional support to individuals and companies on their recruitment needs

Interviewing Skills

Interviewed and pre-screened candidates to assess their fit to job openings available with clients

Sales and Marketing

Achieved sales targets through a customer-focused approach by attracting assignments from key customers on an on-going basis

Training and Development

Conducted relevant HR courses at management school

There are several examples here that can be tightened up. The first few are about including hard evidence in achievements. "Developed a new set of clients" and "created business opportunities" could be transformed into "built £XX worth of new business", and a similar approach throughout would have made this approach less vague (this candidate, in fact, worked for one of India's largest recruitment agencies, and built a huge amount of business with well-known, blue-chip companies). The last line is so vague that it sends out the opposite message to the one intended – at the moment it sounds a little like "I've done at least one course vaguely related to HR in a college you've never heard of, and I can't remember if I finished the course or qualified".

See the further examples below of completed 'Key Achievements and Experience' sections using active language and the 'smart' third person. Note that both of these examples are in the form you would use in profile-led CV, but the way the bullet points are expressed would work equally well in a "straight-in" CV.

Example 'Key Achievements and Experience' from a managerial CV

Key Achievements

Senior Management Experience

- *4yrs+ Managing at site Strategic Senior Team Level*
- *Project managed a £2M project into production, on time and on budget*
- *Managed an Engineering support facility for XYZ Ltd with a repairs and maintenance budget of £95K per year.*

Financial Management

- *Budget Holder and Cost Centre Manager delivering savings annually against budgets for ABC Plc*
- *Initiated cost release programs, saving 20% on direct costs.*

Quality/Customer Focus

- *Initiated & facilitated a site-wide continuous improvement programme at XYZ, realising reduction of 15% of wasted product in Year 1*
- *Delivered measurably high levels of customer satisfaction for products manufactured*
- *Successfully interfaced with internal/external customers and auditors.*

Example 'Key Achievements and Experience' from a graduate CV

Key Achievements and Experience

- *Achieved a work experience placement at XYZ Insurance in the face of strong competition*
- *Gained experience of data analysis with one of Europe's leading firms*
- *College research project on setting up a new membership database for the ABC Institute*
- *Team working to achieve effective joint projects at college*
- *Experience of providing technical support to business users*
- *Communication skills developed by providing 1:1 training in "Computing for the Terrified" at local Adult Education Centre*
- *Self-taught Photoshop user with experience of designing a website displaying photographs*
- *Proficient user of the full range of Microsoft IT packages (including Excel, Access, PowerPoint), and able to exploit its advantages.*

ABOUT ADJECTIVES

Adjectives, if used too often, become an overdose of "look at me". Secondly, CV profiles often use the same tired adjectives as everyone else (virtually every 21-year old claims to be highly motivated, a great communicator and a team player). To use the same old tired language as everyone else makes you undifferentiated, and makes claims the reader finds hard to believe.

The biggest problem is that adjectives don't connect to facts. In our survey several HR managers stressed the need for documents that "contain less self-praise and more objectivity around responsibilities and achievements" and demonstrate "a passion for the area of work, crispness, no waffle, no overblown language".

Skills, adjectives, and evidence

- *"My skills include negotiation ..." sounds like you have just bought a book on negotiation*

- *"I have good negotiation skills" sounds like you might have negotiated something once and felt good about it*

- *"I am a skilled negotiator" sounds as if you're waiting for the idea to be shot down*

- *"I am an effective and proven negotiator" sounds like you could survive at least one round of interview questions on the topic*

- *"I am an exceptional negotiator" is just asking for trouble unless it's swiftly followed up by something that justifies it without question*

- *"My effective negotiation skills put me in the top 10 sales performers in my region" or "Saved 20% on budget through effective negotiation skills" or "I sold more Blockbuster DVD packages than anyone else in the store", although all at different levels, provide a clear link between a claimed skill and actual evidence of achievement.*

HOW DO I RECORD ACHIEVEMENTS IN A LOW STATUS JOB?

Think carefully. Most jobs provide the opportunity to learn, acquire skills, work with others, deal with customers (internal or external), organise and rethink working arrangements, meet targets, and acquire new responsibilities. The problem is usually not the job – people just don't ask enough questions about what they have done. So, instead of listing a fairly typical job as follows:

2002–2006	**Oddjobs Café – Barista/Waiter**
Range of general duties including bar and till work and waiting on tables.	

Try something much more interesting such as:

2002–2006	**Oddjobs Café – Barista/Waiter**

Key experience and achievements:

- *From zero experience, learning within 1 week how to serve the full range of hot beverages*

- *Being allocated Barista duties during the busiest shifts*

- *Training new staff in the use of equipment*

- *Mastering an electronic till – and suggesting some improvements in working practice*

- *Adding to the atmosphere of a lively and successful bar.*

GENERAL GUIDELINES ON RECORDING ACHIEVEMENTS IN ALL CV FORMATS
Presentation style

- Use bullet points, writing in short sentences so that the information is easy to read at a glance.

- Start each bullet point, if possible, with an active verb (e.g. "Changed …").

- Keep most of your bullet points as short as possible, but vary their length.

- Avoid long and complicated phrasing.

- Avoid jargon or technical language.

- Avoid listing skills and outcomes that sound and feel routine or obvious.

- Do not use bullet points to present basic job information or duties.

Content

- Use language that reflects your seniority – don't overstate achievements, but don't undersell them either.

- Where possible, include tangible measures of achievement (profitability, turnover, time or money saved, customer satisfaction ratings, numbers, percentages ...).

- Don't miss out "soft" skills such as negotiating, influencing, coaching and communicating.

- If appropriate, mention the names of well-known organisations.

- Use abbreviated English, in the third person, but avoiding using the words "he" or "she" (e.g. "Introduced call centre environment on shift working basis, re-engineered existing claims processes and new IT systems to fit").

Here's an example of a real set of achievements taken from a CV for an information management specialist. These are set out in the page 1 format you can see discussed in Chapter 8.

KEY ACHIEVEMENTS AND EXPERIENCE

- *Designed and implemented a radically altered company-wide information management system for XYZX consolidating legal, safety and operations information into a single system for multiple users*

- *Created an indexed online system, reducing paper records for ABC by 75%*

- *Refined a condensed information system for approx 22,000 XYZ users*

- *Achieved an MBA in 2002, focusing in my dissertation on the relationship between different parts of a business*

- *Managed a team of 12 data specialists at XYZ, anticipating and meeting training needs*

- *Controlled budgets (of up to £110K pa at XYZ), for premises, microfiche and scanning services*

- *Anticipated the information requirements arising from long-term legal, contractual and environmental obligations*

- *Built a retention schedule to achieve compliance with the Data Protection and Freedom of Information Acts.*

NAMING LEADS TO DOING

There is, in fact, a widely held belief in coaching that hearing, writing and saying these kinds of statements about yourself, your strengths and capabilities has a powerful effect in helping you become more like the person you describe. Just as you are more likely to achieve your goals if you write them down, you're more likely to live out your strengths in an interview. Creating a positive CV helps you to grow into the best version of what you can be.

Completing Your CV

CHAPTER 10

This chapter helps you to:

I Deal with a range of CV writing problems

I Decide what stays in, and what goes out

I Ask frequently asked questions about CV writing

I Undertake a final review of layout and style

"Let each become all that he was created capable of being."

Thomas Carlyle

FINALISING YOUR CV

Having decided on your CV format and written up much of the key information about your work history and skills, you will find that there are still some areas of the CV that will need writing, and some problems that are common to all CV formats.

How long should my CV be?

Over-long CVs often indicate insecurity. If you say too much at interview you run the risk of talking yourself out of the job. Saying too much on your CV can look like a lack of focus on what you are looking for and what you have to offer. In most situations, anything more than three pages starts to get counter-productive. Do remember the impact of the first page – getting the first page right is vital, and is more important than trimming a three-page CV down to two pages.

Our CV research indicates that most employers are happy with a CV that is two or three pages long. One HR specialist wrote that "I think that people appreciate that they need to be more concise and so the length has got shorter but the downside is that as a result many candidates try too hard to make an impact".

Be guided by what is considered the norm in your sector. A marketing CV will rarely be more than two pages, while an academic CV may be very long indeed if it lists a large range of publications.

Do I need to give my CV a title?

Don't title it "Curriculum Vitae". The title of the document is your name, in a slightly larger, bold font, followed by your contact details. Placing this information in the centre of the page looks good.

What's the best way to present my contact details?

Although this seems a very obvious point, double check each digit of your telephone numbers and each character of your email address. A recruiter will only make one attempt to reach you. Print your name in the exact form you want it to be used in interview. Otherwise you begin your document by misdirecting your reader. If your name is Alexander Benjamin Smith but everyone calls you Ben, then simply put "Ben Smith" in large letters across the top of the CV. When putting in contact information, keep it simple and appropriate. If you include an email address and a mobile number, make sure you check for messages daily. Setting up a voicemail on your home number which you can check while you are travelling is also a good idea. Often candidates give only a mobile number, which again is not a problem if you have voicemail.

What about email addresses?

A CV without an email address is asking for trouble – it broadcasts the fact that you don't know or don't care about modern technology. Make sure the email address is user friendly (not "dgi8cg28@1*?_a.com") and business-like rather than humorous ("ben.smith@example.com") rather than "bensmiffy" or "madbenny" or "housewifey" or any of the other endearing addresses we love to use with our friends. It's relatively easy to use multiple email addresses with the messages all ending up in one account – but be careful which one you reply from, as your sending address will appear in your message. Confirming an interview as "bennyairhead" may not be the best start to a successful relationship with your new employer. Where you are including an email address in a CV that will be submitted electronically, you should make sure that this is included as an actual link in your Word document.

Should I include a target job statement?

There are some circumstances when you might include a "target job" statement on a CV. At one stage recruiters encouraged candidates to put this boldly at the header of a CV, e.g. "Target Job – Retail Manager". This is rarely a good idea, as discussed in the disadvantages below. A better alternative is to include an indication of your ideal or target job in the last line of your profile, e.g." Currently seeking to build on retail management skills in a challenging new environment that will give increased opportunities for staff management and training". (See also Chapter 8 on including a Target Job Statement in a profile.)

How far back should I go when listing jobs?

The main rule here is clarity of message. If you did a very important job 30 years ago that shaped your whole CV, you need to mention it. However, if your past contains few surprises it's probably not important to list every role you've undertaken since you left full-time education. Doing so often gives unnecessary emphasis to your age.

It probably doesn't make sense to provide detailed information about jobs you did more than 10–15 years ago, but don't make the mistake of leaving them out – recruitment consultants in particular get rather concerned about gaps in your CV. Simply listing each role, organisation and dates will do for older jobs or you can go for a blanket statement, e.g. "1980–1988 Engineering Apprenticeship, followed by a range of positions as Electronic Engineer". In the event that an employer wants more precise details, you can provide it.

Should I include reasons for job change?

There is no requirement to give reasons for job change in your CV itself, and volunteering your reasons on paper usually means asking for trouble. However, do be prepared to answer this question at interview.

If you were dismissed from a role at any stage in the past you may be legally required to state this on an application form or if asked a direct question at interview. There is, however, no obligation for you to volunteer the information in a CV. If you changed jobs because you couldn't stand your boss or hated the organisation then keep it to yourself – that information should never go anywhere near a recruiter.

Should I mention the fact I was made redundant?

Similarly, there is no reason to mention redundancy on a CV (although sometimes it's helpful especially if you only had a short spell in one job or a long job-search period). Do prepare yourself for questions about it at interview. Remember that redundancy is now an experience shared by people in all sectors and of all ages, and is not a social stigma or a sign that you are dispensable. The best way to deal with it at interview is quickly, moving the conversation on to the future: "As you know, XYZ went through a restructuring process, and like many people at I was laid off this year. This has given me a good opportunity to rethink my career options and I am now very focused on the kind of job that would really suit me ...".

How do I deal with gaps in my CV?

There is no point trying to hide gaps in your work history. It's one of the first things a recruiter looks for. Make sure you cover each relevant period of your work history. If you don't, a recruiter may assume all the wrong things, such as a long and difficult job-search period or lack of focus and direction. Here are some of the main reasons why you might have CV gaps, and some ways of dealing with them:

1. **Job-search periods** – if you did any work at all, list it, but if you have a significant gap, which can only be explained by reference to job search, write as positively as you can, e.g. "an interesting job-search period where I became very clear about my working goals and had the opportunity to meet and investigate a wide range of organisations".

2. **Undertaking temporary work** – this may well provide tremendous opportunities to write about transferable skills and sectoral knowledge. Consider each temporary job as a piece of work experience. Write briefly about what you got out of each role and how it has added to your employability.

3. **Study** – there is no reason to leave this out. If it was study around a subject that is not strictly related to your career, spell out the transferable skills acquired.

4. **Travel** – a great opportunity to write about what you did, what you learned and how you did it.

5. **Family commitments** – you may have had to take time out because of child care or because of other family commitments. Here again, being absolutely straight about what you did (and possibly referring to what you learned in the process) is far better than leaving a blank.

6. **Career break** – these are becoming increasingly common. Negotiating a career break and doing something interesting may be what makes you distinctive. See Chapter 4 for more on this topic.

7. **Going off track** – there are many ways of wandering off track, some of them listed above. Others might include periods of illness, serving a prison sentence or taking time out for other reasons. Start by being clear about what you *have* to say legally. Then do whatever you can to demonstrate, if the impact is negative, a simple message: that was then, this is now. Work even harder to demonstrate your ability and commitment.

Should I mention my current or last salary?

A number of recruiters and employers will tell you that they find it useful to know what you have been earning, because it's a rough guide to whether the role is right for you. However, including your salary details on a CV can lead to problems. Doing so may immediately rule you out where an employer has in mind a significantly lower salary than you have received. Equally, if the prospective salary is a lot more than you are currently receiving, your current pay level may be taken as an indicator of your ability. On balance, it's best to keep salary information off your CV. Dealing with the question verbally once you have already got a certain way into the process gives you a far greater chance of resolving any difficulties.

Do I have to list the dates of each job?

There is great confusion in the marketplace at the moment about whether you should include dates against each job. Some employers believe that they should not seek this information. Others find it useful and believe they are allowed to seek such information, as long as they do not use it to discriminate on the grounds of age. Some employers will wish to check your work history anyway as part of a reference checking procedure, and may want to see original copies of certificates and qualifications.

You are not required to include dates of any kind in a CV. However, you run the risk of your CV being excluded if you do not include the start and end dates for each job. Our CV survey shows that 97% of employers still want to see information about the dates you were employed. Normally this will be set out in years (e.g. 2000–2003), although for very recent jobs you may want to identify the actual start and finish months (e.g. March 2006–January 2007). Keep a record of your exact employment dates separately – it's useful for tax purposes.

How long employers are allowed to consider date-related information is a matter for speculation. The current interpretation of the law is that employers may ask for this information and you can supply it, but an employer must not use such information to discriminate against you unfairly.

My work experience is a jumble sale – what do I do?

This is where a lot of people begin. Their qualifications don't relate to their work history, their most recent job is a distraction and taken together the listed jobs seem to bear no relationship with each other. The problem is that if you haven't made any kind of sense of your CV, no one else will. Don't apologise in your CV or covering letter, but try to make the document itself make sense of what you've done. Remember that people change jobs much more frequently than they used to and it's now far more acceptable to demonstrate variety and unusual backgrounds in your CV. If you are going to make sense of it, you will probably need to use a profile-led CV (see Chapter 7), and possibly also a separate list of skills. The main thing is to work out some kind of pattern or coherence; for example, you may discover that all of your jobs have been about motivating people or solving problems or providing excellent customer service. If so, bring that point out in your profile and relate it to the kind of job you'd like to do next.

How do I deal with complex job titles and job functions?

Remember the likely reader. Explain unusual roles or titles in plain English, and briefly. Too many CVs lose their way because they use undigested jargon or get into overcomplicated terminology. Learn how to write simple straightforward English, e.g.: "**Customer Service Advisor** – my job was to provide speedy, efficient and friendly response to consumer complaints by telephone and letter".

Many HR staff would agree with the CV survey respondent who complained of "Increasing use of jargon – which usually indicates that the writer has failed to think about the reader and their need to understand".

What about overseas jobs?

There is no reason why you shouldn't gain brownie points in your CV by writing about work in other countries. It can provide supporting evidence of cross-cultural experience, language skills or breadth of experience. Do ensure that you make it clear where you want to work *now*, or an employer may assume that you'd rather pursue an international career. And do translate foreign job titles or terminology into user-friendly English.

How much should I say about my educational history?

You are not *required* to include dates when you attended school, college or university, or the dates when you achieved your qualifications. However, our CV survey shows that 60% of employers want to know the date you became qualified.

What far too many CVs do, however, is to give unnecessary information about where you were educated. Some employers might be influenced by what they perceive to be a "good" university (and the name of the business school where you obtained your MBA is very important). However, few recruiters or employers want to see the name of your primary or secondary school.

With qualifications, just list those and also grades that you think will be of interest to an employer. Often the whole question of qualifications is an unstated one: "will you have the thinking skills to cope with the training and the job?". As this is often benchmarked in very broad terms, phrases such as "graduate" or "A Level standard" will sometimes do the job. In most cases, list any qualifications you have obtained at or above A Level or the equivalent. See Chapter 3 for more dos and don'ts on qualifications.

Try to say something user friendly and interesting about your main qualifications. A subject title is rarely helpful to an employer. A recruiter makes assumptions about the usefulness of your qualifications unless you specifically state what you most enjoyed, what special projects you undertook and what you got out of your studies as a whole.

Often what organisations are checking is that minimum standards have been achieved. You may achieve this simply by including the word "graduate" in your profile. If you haven't got a degree, then make sure that the first page of your CV talks about evidence that convinces a reader that you have achieved the same standard, e.g. work experience, training courses attended, on-the-job training.

Should I mention "offbeat" qualifications or courses?

This rather depends on what you mean by "offbeat" – what will be off-putting in one sector may be intriguing to another. Mention them if they add to the picture or at least communicate something of your motivation outside work. Don't mention them if experience tells you that they scream out "wrong kind of person".

How should I mention a PhD?

A lot of recruiters I have interviewed in the past have expressed their irritation for a non-medical CV that uses the term "Dr". Unless having this qualification is the norm, or gives you a particular advantage, it seems wise to resist writing "Dr" at the top of your CV, but do mention "PhD" in your list of qualifications, and give as much useful details as you can about what makes it relevant – e.g. the challenges you overcame, the expertise and niche knowledge it has provided. Consider missing it out if feedback tells you that you appear overqualified for your target roles.

How do I write a CV if I have just left full-time education with little real work experience?

This is a question commonly asked by those who are just about to leave school, college or university. Begin by analysing every job (no matter how short term) or work-related activity including work placements, work shadowing, visits to workplaces, etc. Next, think deep and hard about your life achievements (including things you have done in your studies, your social life). Give strong emphasis to the adventurous, unusual or risk-taking, including travel and gap years. Look at your activities outside study. Perhaps you organised complicated or exciting social events, competitions or sporting activities, or you may have been a member of a society or club. Think about the transferable skills that you acquired from these all experiences, and make sure that they are mentioned in your CV.

Tips for CV writing for those leaving full-time education (Particularly those with limited work experience)

- Profile

  Avoid the predictable. Almost every university and college leaver claims to be highly motivated, a team player and in possession of great communication skills. Also resist claims you can't support. Give a clear, straightforward summary of your experience and success to date (see Chapter 8 for more details)

- Experience

  Talk about your past as much as your potential. Write about relevant experience (e.g. work, travel, time out). Indicate what kind of challenges you faced, what you learned and what you achieved

- Skills

  Be honest, avoiding empty claims and undue modesty. Identify your skills and state your level of competence. Give examples of what you have done with these skills and what you achieved

- Key achievements

  Think about your accomplishments in different contexts: study, work, leisure time and voluntary activities. Use bullet points to list times you made an impact. Try to present your achievements in concrete, measurable terms

- Qualifications

  Explain, translate, communicate. Don't assume that an employer is automatically interested in your academic achievements. Don't over-emphasise poor results

- Continuing professional development and training

  Don't forget to include details about non-academic courses and training, even if they are uncertificated. If you have the skills but not the qualifications, give an indication of what you have achieved with them (e.g. producing a complex spreadsheet)

- Work history

  Even if your history is limited, what did you actually do? What problems did you solve? Look at any work you have ever done and find a way to communicate the skills you used and the contribution you made

- Support skills

  Think about the support skills you can offer, and an employer's expectations (e.g. IT, word processing, customer service or sales skills). Don't miss out anything, particularly IT skills. Indicate your standard of competence

- Fields of work

  Work out what kind of work interests you. Communicate enthusiasm to employers: show them that you really want to work in their field, not that they happen to be the first to have a vacancy

- Interests

  Include a good range. An employer won't expect you to have a long work history, but will expect you to be a rounded person with an interesting life outside work. Think of interests and activities that include other people or draw upon skills that may be relevant to work.

How much detail should I give about training?

Writing about your training is generally good news on a CV, even if the training didn't lead to a qualification. It can demonstrate motivation (to get onto a course, to succeed), a clear learning agenda, skill acquisition and development, and career direction. Don't just list the name of all the courses you've attended, but focus on the ones that matter and say something interesting about them. Explain any training courses that may not be clear to the reader, e.g.:

> *2007 "Star Trainer" course* – a 5-day "Train the Trainer" course, final certificate awarded by assessment of a live training event plus independent 360-degree feedback from course trainees.

What kind of personal information should I include?

In the kind of CV you would write for the UK market it's unlikely that you will include very much personal information. Some of this information is material that employers aren't allowed to ask about anyway, and most of it is irrelevant to the key function of the CV – getting you in the interview room. You should not provide details of your marital status, number or ages of children, or any family members who are dependent on you.

You are *not* required to include your age or date of birth on your CV. Do remember, however, that other things in your CV may give the game away, e.g. the date you graduated or completed an apprenticeship, or the ages of adult children.

For some roles it helps to mention if you have a full driving licence and if you are a car owner. If you need, and possess, permission to work in the UK, state this (or your visa status) clearly.

Should I mention my interests?

My advice on this point hasn't changed over the years. Do try to say something that gives a picture of a person who has a life outside work. If you can mention interests that have some relevance to the workplace, brilliant. If you can mention interests that draw upon and maintain relevant skills, also excellent. Otherwise, don't list any interests that you are not prepared to talk about with some enthusiasm. And although one employer admitted an aversion to "scary or unusual hobbies", resist the identikit, bland list seen by too many HR departments: *restaurants, theatre, walking* ... . One employer in our survey complained of "Too much irrelevant personal information – e.g. names of children, interests such as 'reading', 'travel' – we all read and travel!". In contrast, another HR manager admitted her worry about "candidates with no life outside work".

Do I provide references?

A small number of recruiters like to see the names of referees printed on the end of your CV. Generally, this is best avoided. Our survey indicates that only a minority of HR departments expect to see references listed on your CV.

Your CV may be copied, forwarded by email and generally passed along without your knowledge. You may not know when or why your referees are being approached. Try to keep a fairly tight lid on this: be clear when references are going to be obtained and brief your referees what the job is all about (reminding them, if it's appropriate, which parts of your experience offer a reasonable match, and send your referee an up-to-date copy of your CV to help jog their memory).

You can say "References Are Available on Request", but it wastes a line on your CV. References will be asked for if an employer needs them. End of story. If an employer asks you to provide the names of referees when you apply, you can always add them to your covering letter.

Should I mention health problems?

You are not required to provide information about health problems on a CV, or even a statement of your general health. If you are asked direct questions about your health history at interview or in an application form, you must answer them honestly and accurately. Employers will typically ask about health conditions if you are being offered medical or health insurance, or being considered for a company pension scheme. You may, for example, be asked how many days' sick leave you had in the past 1 or 2 years.

I can't get my CV to match the role. What do I do?

Often what's required here is better mining for evidence. Go back to the **Role Analysis Sheet** in Chapter 6. Having done that, if you still find it difficult to match your CV to the *key* requirements of the role, then the role probably isn't for you. There's no point distorting reality or falsifying information in order to get an interview. If you put a false slant on your CV information you will be unlikely to provide the necessary supporting evidence at interview. Even more worrying, you might get the job. In the end, recruitment is about matching people to jobs. There are enough people out there struggling in jobs they are badly suited to without adding yourself to the pile.

CV Survey Top Tips on CV Layout and Style

The HR specialists who responded to the CV research programme outlined in Chapter 2 were asked what they preferred to see in a CV. Here are their top 10 tips on CV layout and style.

1. *"Clarity of layout – ease of navigation around the CV."*
2. *"Be punchy, concise and attention grabbing"*
3. *"Well spaced with short sentences"*
4. *"Key achievements listed per position held"*
5. *"An overall summary statement confirming what you have achieved and what you are looking for"*
6. *"Plain English – no buzz words"*
7. *"Clear indication of career progression/history from end of education to current date"*
8. *"White space on the page and bullet point information"*
9. *"Visually easy to read – not too 'word heavy'. Perfect spelling and grammar!"*
10. *"All contact information available on first page".*

Integrating Your Message Into a Multi-strategy Job Search

This chapter helps you to:

▌ Build on your CV

▌ Understand the essentials of a multi-strategy job search

▌ Anticipate how your CV will be used in a job interview

▌ Plan for questions that probe your CV evidence

▌ Spot in advance the weak spots in your interview performance

"Think like a wise man but communicate in the language of the people."
William Butler Yeats

AN INTEGRATED APPROACH

This book has attempted to put some key stages in place to help you find a job that closely matches who you are and what you have to offer. It has focused on getting your message right, and doing so at that critical stage – CV writing – where you can easily be lost in a sea of hopeful applicants.

It would be easy to make the mistake of thinking that writing the strongest possible CV is all you need to do to net a brilliant job. It's a key step, because if you get through a paper sift you move close enough to an organisation to make an impact, personally. A CV can also be a useful back-up tool to remind people of things you have said during a networking meeting. However, you will also need to use all the tools and techniques at your disposal to make the time you put into your job search as effective as possible.

Job searching on several levels at once

To get the best out of your new CV, think about how you are going to use it. If you want an average career, follow the herd and adopt an average job search. It's too easy to settle for playing the job market by lottery rules. For example, if you just chase advertised jobs you may be up against 500-plus other applicants. With those odds, it doesn't matter if you have the best CV in the world. Rejection leads to loss of confidence, and it's easy to start trashing your goals.

Effective career changers know that a multi-strategy approach works best.

Five Steps to a multi-strategy job search

1. Build up a strong relationship with at least six and up to 20 **recruitment consultancies**. Make sure they understand what you're really looking for by communicating your "why you" message as often as possible.

2. Learn how to interrogate **job advertisements**, matching your strengths to an employer's shortlist in a brief, highly focused covering letter. Sometimes you will also need to complete application forms (see the item later in this chapter).

3. Use the **Internet**, particularly the better job boards and organisations' own sites, but don't waste time on the Internet during working hours when you can be following steps 4 and 5. (See Chapter 14 for advice on using your CV online.)

4. Investigate your choices by **talking to people** about what's out there. Go to the edge of your comfort zone when it comes to networking, and keep asking the question "who else should I be talking to?". Enthusiasm and a hunger to find new outlets for your talents gets you noticed in the hidden (i.e. unadvertised) job market.

5. Target organisations directly with a well-pitched letter and CV. These **speculative approaches** to organisations can be surprisingly effective – if you have a good covering letter and a strong CV. This method works surprisingly well if your approach is carefully targeted. (See Chapter 13 for tips on writing speculative letters.)

Whatever you do, don't miss out Step 4. You learn more and get greater breakthroughs through talking to people. Research sectors by asking around, not through web pages. Find out where your skills will be valued, which organisations can offer you the right kind of challenge or learning opportunity and (particularly important) the organisations that are doing things you believe in.

RESEARCH BEFORE YOU JOB SEARCH

Don't fire your new CV off in all directions. Find out what's out there through networking (see below) and by undertaking background research. The Internet is a fantastic tool for this purpose, but don't undervalue word of mouth advice.

In March 2007 the Royal Bank of Scotland analysed the amount of time that graduates spend planning their careers. The RBS Career Start Report stated that nearly a third of final-year students had spent less than a day researching their potential career, while just a quarter say they had spent more than 5 days looking into it. Even less time was spent researching specific employers. Nearly half of the students polled, all of whom had applied for graduate programmes, admitted they spent less than a couple of hours researching a particular company before they applied for a job. No wonder then that nearly 50% said they didn't expect to stay in their graduate job longer than 2 years.

Accepting a permanent job is a decision that could affect the next 10 years of your life. It will have an impact on security, learning, lifestyle, and relationships in and out of work. You wouldn't enter into any other kind of 10-year relationship on the strength of half an hour's research plus a 45-minute interview. Research in order to get an interview, keep on researching to help you get the job and research again (ideally talking to previous and current employees) if a job offer is on the table.

MAKING THE MOST OF RECRUITMENT CONSULTANCIES

Recruitment consultants can help your job search in many ways, but do remember that they are usually vacancy-driven – they have jobs to fill. This means that they are hunting for evidence of a simple, immediate match between job and candidate. This is the reason why you may need to use a profile-led CV with a recruiter, even though they may react against it. If you offer a "straight-in" CV you may end up in exactly the pigeon-hole you want to avoid.

Recruitment consultants can give you all kinds of useful information – about the state of the market, about local opportunities, about your interview technique. They will undoubtedly also want to give you advice on your CV. In the UK recruitment consultancies, whatever their label, are not allowed to charge a fee to job seekers for finding them work. They can, however, charge a fee for a separate service such as producing a CV for you, but when they do this they should give you clear written terms of business when asking for your money.

Recruitment consultants and the "straight-in" CV

Often a recruitment consultant can give you feedback on your CV, and on your overall "message". As recruiters often have strong views on CV layout, take this advice with some caution and take other opinions as well. Every recruiter has pet likes and dislikes when it comes to CVs, which usually relate to the kind of candidates that they place most often. It's fair to say that most recruitment consultants prefer the 'straight-in" CV. They often claim that a profile or skills summary gets in the way of hard evidence, and they want to get as quickly as possible to the "meat" of your CV. The following views therefore need to be presented to communicate some of the problems you experience using a profile-led CV.

"No Objective Statement, No Personal Profile" is the hard and fast rule of experienced recruiter and business consultant Jeff Grout, author of *Recruiting Excellence*. For Grout, the "profile" in a CV is "purely subjective – the candidate is not going to say anything negative about themselves – and disregarded by most recruiters".

Joëlle Warren, Managing Director of Warren Partners Executive Search, writes: "I don't like profile paragraphs. My first response is 'says who?' – the only person I've ever allowed to include one was a head teacher and he included a quote from OFSTED about his leadership which I classified as more a 'proof statement'. I've never come across one that says 'surly, negative, who cheeses off his team', so they become meaningless. As far as a list of achievements is concerned I prefer seeing them against each role but what I do encourage on page 1 is to make sure there's a flavour of the whole career. So, for example, if they are a MD but from a financial background and the financial roles are further back on the CV, or if they are currently at an SME but have a background in blue chips, I would recommend they include a career summary on the front page so that there is a 'flavour' of the CV encapsulated on page one and it doesn't need to be dug around for".

Another recruiter states in a list of CV tips: "Please, no personal introduction describing in a surfeit of adjectives how wonderful you are. An experienced recruiter never reads it; they are the ones who are expected to assess your ability, not you".

Top 10 tips for the "straight-in" CV aimed at a recruitment consultant

1. It should be between two and three pages. Any longer and it will not be read, too short and key evidence will be missing.

2. Start with your (brief) personal and contact details.

3. Do not write a profile. Recruiters are happy for you to outline the type of challenge you are looking for, and explain why you want it, in a brief covering letter.

4. Put your current job first, and use reverse chronology throughout.

5. Head up each new job in bold font, setting out clearly your job titles, organisation names and relevant dates.

6. Use upper and lower case headings, which are easier to read than capitals

7. After each job is listed explain the role and context in a few sentences.

8. List major successes in each job under the heading "Major Achievements", followed by between three and six bullet points conveying your strengths (see Chapter 9).

9. Repeat the same format as you work through previous jobs, but make each progressively shorter.

10. Include interests and personal activities at the end – recruiters are interested in this information.

USING A PROFILE-LED CV WITH RECRUITMENT CONSULTANTS

This chapter has already rehearsed the fact that a number of recruitment consultants do not take warmly to a profile-led CV and prefer what this book describes as the "straight-in" model. However, even taking the above views into account, sometimes you want to use a profile-led CV (e.g. because you want to change sector or because you want your CV to convey a particular message – see Chapter 4). If you feel the need to present a profile-led CV to a recruitment consultant, use the following tips to improve acceptability.

Top tips for the profile-led CV aimed at a recruitment consultant

1. Make sure the profile is short, punchy, and free of flowery adjectives and other irritating features including empty claims (see Chapter 8).

2. Make sure that you create space to include details of your present job on page 1 (this may mean cutting the Career Summary, Achievements Section or both).

3. Avoid using a Career Summary unless it's vital to your cause.

4. Mention sector experience somewhere in the profile.

5. Make sure that your profile in a CV aimed at a recruiter makes it very clear which new sector you are aiming for, and why.

6. If listing a summarised set of skills and achievements, find some way of linking them to specific jobs (e.g. "Organised, at XYZ Ltd, a new Intranet-based customer service system").

NETWORKING YOUR WAY INTO A JOB INTERVIEW

In order to find potential targets for your CV you need to have a clear sense of the options available. That's where lateral thinking comes in. If you were a company in crisis, you'd be thinking about new markets, new clients. The career parallel is that you need to know what's out there. Trying to plan a career change without information about fields of work is like trying to plan a journey with a blank road map.

Do your homework about sectors and likely employers. New kinds of jobs are being created all the time. Look at the jobs around you, and ask how many of them existed 25 years ago. Who in 1985 would have recognised the term "e-learning consultant"? Every new invention, every development in technology, means brand new job titles. Finding out about work sectors ultimately also means talking to real people about the jobs they do – the first step to successful networking.

Taking a fresh look isn't just about collecting data. It's also about using lateral thinking to spot the possible links between what you already know and where you want to be. The main thing is to keep focused on *why* you are networking. You're not doing it just as an excuse to put your CV under someone's nose. The first function of networking is exploration – finding out who and what is out there. The second function (which happens as a spin-off) is that you become visible in the hidden (unadvertised) job market. By finding out, and by asking smart questions, you become perceived as a credible candidate. It's at that point, when someone has a clear idea of your overall personal brand, that you leave a strong, well-focused CV as a reminder.

If you want to get the most out of networking, find a good careers coach, if you can. At the very least, recruit some positive-thinking friends to support you through your exploration, your discoveries, and to help you cope with the ups and downs of finding the right people.

SPECULATIVE APPROACHES

Don't underestimate the value of a well-targeted speculative approach, sending your CV to an employer who is not advertising at the moment but might have need of your expertise. See Chapter 13 for examples of well-constructed speculative letters.

COMPLETING APPLICATION FORMS

If you have completed some of the foundational exercises in this book and have details of your work history, skills and experience on your PC, you will find it relatively straightforward (although very time-consuming) to fill in an application form. Sometimes this can be done online; sometimes this still has to be done on paper. If you can cut and paste information do so, but proof-read very carefully – it is all too easy to leave in information about another employer.

Tips when completing an application form
Preparation

- Photocopy the form before you write anything on it.

- Read the form and its instructions carefully.

- Read the Job Description thoroughly. Try to work out what problem the job is there to solve.

- Carefully note any key competences or qualities.

- Make sure that you do not miss out key information that might be used to screen completed forms, e.g. qualifications, experience, technical skills … .

- Use a highlighter pen on a copy of your CV to pick out relevant achievements or examples.

Completing the application form

- If completing the form by hand use black ink. Write legibly.

- Try to leave some white space around text so the completed form is still visually pleasing rather than cramped and over-full.

- Use bullet points where appropriate.

- Remember that the completed form will be read at high speed. Emphasise key information.

- Make positive statements relating to your skills and achievements.

- Write only a brief covering letter unless you are asked to put particular information in the letter itself. Use the letter to remind the reader how you match the key requirements of the job.

- Regard a section with a heading such as "Other Information" as an opportunity to sell yourself.

Checking and submitting the form

- Always photocopy the completed form for your records.

- Complete the form promptly, and make sure it is returned by the deadline.

- It can be a good idea to telephone to confirm safe receipt of your application form. If there is any doubt, send a copy.

DRAWING ON YOUR CV AT INTERVIEW

If your CV is successful, it will give you the opportunity to attend an interview. This is your chance to support and build on the evidence presented in your CV. Once you've won the interview, the main thing that matters is that you demonstrate both the right experience and potential. What's even more important is that you **don't talk yourself out of the job**.

Interview preparation

The art of presenting your experience well at interview is to do your planning work in advance, and not to try to recall useful examples in the interview room itself. To be well-armed with short, clear examples you should begin with your CV. Examine all the information which is available to you about the job. Look at the CV you used to get the interview. Pick out the evidence in your CV that most clearly matches the employer's shopping list of skills, competencies, knowledge and other aspects including personality. Be prepared, with evidence, to answer questions which probe details in your CV. Even more importantly, be prepared to supply examples that are *not* included in your CV. Respond with detail, but *not too much*. The interviewer may be happy with your initial response if it is focused. Saying too much increases the chance of introducing negative ideas and information.

Questions about your Profile

If your profile makes claims that are not supported elsewhere in your CV then expect some tough questions. Prepare the kind of evidence that should have appeared in your CV – strong evidence supporting the claim that these are things you have done, not just ambitions.

Your profile may begin with a word or phrase that describes you in a nutshell, perhaps in terms of a job title or professional summary (e.g. "an experienced marketing executive"). If the job you are being interviewed for isn't an automatic match for that description be prepared to explain why you want to change sector, and how you might convince an employer that your skills are transferable. If your profile includes a target job, be prepared for questions that ask how much flexibility you have around this goal, or questions that probe your ambition or future career plans.

Questions about your Work History

Remember that the perfect interview intends to gain sufficient information about your past experience in order to **try to predict your future workplace performance**. Interviewers are quizzing you in order to gain insights into your professional experiences – the projects and tasks you have handled, your past working relationships, your successes and problems.

Be prepared to talk about positions you have held, what you learned from them, and be specific about job titles, dates and job responsibilities. Keep it interesting, and try to talk about something that connects all the jobs you've done – possibly something about what you have learned or what the jobs have in common. Be consistent about details, particularly dates and job titles. If an interviewer feels you are being evasive or hiding something you will quickly talk yourself out of the job.

Anticipating the line of questioning

There are reliable ways of guessing where an interviewer is going to probe. Likely areas will be:

- Gaps in your work history.

- Where you have listed qualifications without indicating final grades.

- Where you have made unsupported claims.

- Where your competencies appear to be at a level significantly lower or higher than those required by the job.

- Specific examples of achievements.

- High and low points in your career.

- How you work under pressure.

- Personal strengths and weaknesses.

- Where you lack experience in a role or sector.

- Reasons for leaving jobs in the past.

Questions about your Skills

If your CV has got you this far, it will have presented a catalogue of your skills. Be prepared, with more evidence than you need, for further probing questions. Do your homework by spotting what you believe to be the top six to eight competencies in a job. Go back to Chapter 9 (on achievements) to prepare further evidence of times when you exercised particular skills, exactly what you did and what happened as a result.

Questions about your Personality

If you have made claims about your personality (outgoing, dependable, self-starting, …) and working style (creative, organised, meticulous, …) be prepared to give supporting evidence at interview, particularly if your CV lacks hard and fast evidence or includes examples that are not strongly related to the job in question.

Questions about your Qualifications

If you have failed to include grades or other details expect interviewers to ask you to fill the gap. If your results were less than promising, be prepared to answer questions on your academic performance. It's perhaps more likely that an interviewer will skip over your qualifications or not ask about them at all. If you have strong skills that you acquired during your studies, be prepared to use the evidence here.

Creating the idea that your CV has a theme or pattern

Try, as far as is reasonable, to link elements in your CV together into a coherent whole: "I think there's a thread that links all the jobs that

I've done, and it's an interest in developing people. I started my working life as a lecturer, but then moved through a series of commercial training roles. More recently I've managed a training department and commissioned a number of major new projects. Perhaps it would help if I tell you a little about the job I've done most recently …".

Questions about your interests

You should only have included interests in your CV if they pass one of two tests: (a) you could, if pressed, talk enthusiastically about this interest for 10 minutes or more, or (b) the interest presents qualities or skills that are relevant to the job. Focus on the second area.

A word about jargon

The use of technical language can be a way of showing that you speak the right "code". However, as our CV survey indicates, many recruiting employers find jargon off-putting and an alienating kind of "insider" language. If you want to use jargon, be sure you are current and up to date, and be prepared for probing questions designed to check that you really understand what you are talking about. You may, of course, need to respond to some jargon being used by an interviewer to check if you really know your stuff. Generally, it's better to speak in plain English – it certainly communicates your ability to explain your job to non-specialists.

Limiting your answers

Don't let your answers become monologues. Ideal answers last between 30 seconds and 2 minutes. Don't feel the need to tell your life story – interviewers "tune out" very quickly.

Anticipating rejection

Practice your interview techniques with experienced recruiters. It's important to anticipate setbacks. There are many reasons why you won't be successful at interview, and most of them have nothing to do with you. Often employers change their mind about what they are looking for or get distracted by certain issues or sometimes they already have an individual in mind for the job.

Planning to deal with rejection from the outset is critical; if you let the first "thank, but no thanks" letter put you off, it's easy to trash the whole plan. If you conduct any kind of job search most experiences will be negative, because you need to shift a lot of earth to find a diamond. Planning for rejection is another above-average strategy.

This last step is the most important. Think positively about yourself, and create a small support team around you to do the same thing. It's the only way of getting past the psychological barriers blocking you – the internal voices that tell you that you are too old, underqualified, the wrong kind of person ... . Most of the barriers are ones you create yourself.

For further interview tips including methods for preparing for competency-based interviews, see Job Interviews: Top Answers to Tough Questions *by John Lees and Matthew DeLuca (McGraw-Hill, 2004).*

If you want to think about networking in detail you may find it useful to see the sections on informational interviewing outlined in How To Get A Job You'll Love.

Getting Through a Competency Screening Process

This chapter helps you to:

I Adapt your CV for a competency-based recruitment process

I Deliver your message in the right language and structure

I Communicate your competencies in a convincing way

I Plan for competency-based interviews

"It is by acts and not by ideas that people live."

Anatole France

MAKING SURE YOUR CV WORKS ON A COMPETENCY-BASED SIFT

We have already looked, in Chapter 11, at the importance of preparing for an interview that will use your CV as a starting point. We turn now to a slightly more demanding selection and interview process.

What is competency-based selection?

A competency is, in its simplest form, a set of "performance behaviours". One of the proponents of this idea was Professor Richard Boyatzis, who defined a competency as "an underlying characteristic of an individual which is causally related to effective or superior performance".

A competency is therefore not just a skill, but is a combination of know-how, skills, attitude and demonstrated behaviours – all directed towards outcomes that actively assist an employer. A competency is not just about what you do, but how you do it.

A simple example is answering the telephone. A competent operator will be able to answer a telephone within a prescribed number of rings and deal efficiently with a customer. An above-average performer will display competency by also making the customer feel informed and valued. This particular competency might be defined as "Building and maintaining customer relationships on the telephone".

This description is typical of a competency. Others for someone in a customer service role might be:

- Handling multiple tasks under time pressure.

- The ability to manage and prioritise your own workload.

- Dealing with demanding or difficult customers.

- Improvising solutions.

In our CV survey, 56% of employers stated that they would like to see competencies listed on CVs. One respondent specifically likes to see "Differentiating specialist skills and competencies".

Responding to a competency-based selection process

This task is essentially about decoding – analysing job information to see how competencies are being used. There are a number of ways that competency-based selection can be applied by a recruiting organisation. As you can see from the following list of typical contexts, sometimes the fact that competencies are being discussed is far from clear as far as candidates are concerned.

Competency evidence may be sought:

- Where competencies are clearly stated by the employer and it is made clear how each competency will be measured. In this case you will almost certainly be asked to write **competency statements** (see below).

- Where competencies are clearly stated by the employer and it is not clear how each competency will be measured. In this case you need to highlight your competencies in your (adapted) CV and in your covering letter.

- Where stated competencies will be measured alongside other factors. This again requires evidence in your CV and letter.

- Where unstated competencies will be measured alongside other factors. There is only a small amount you can do in advance here – by trying to work out the likely competencies required, and making sure your CV covers these areas.

- Where unstated competencies will be measured in a fairly unstructured way. The only way to prepare for this is to think in advance about how you will sell your competencies at interview (see later in this chapter).

- Where a discussion of competencies might come up informally during an interview. Again, having a few prepared statements ready for interview will be a bonus.

Matching your experience to the evidence

Look carefully at any information you can find about competencies that are considered ess*ential or useful for the job*. You can, obviously, spot these where specific competencies are listed and *defined by the organisation*. You may be given a written statement listing the competencies and inviting you to give detailed information about times where you have used them. You may find that the advertisement and job description talk about a mix of skills, knowledge, attitudes and behaviours – in other words, competencies. Alternatively, the job may be defined in terms of activities, targets or outcomes – work back from those to establish what kind of behaviours will be needed to achieve them.

Even when it comes to basic competencies, make sure you have good examples and detail. For example, if you are talking about filing as a competency, identify a time when you dealt with something difficult or unusual. Look at the clues available to you about job content, and (from the Job Description or your own judgement) work out the five or six competencies that seem to be the most important in this role. Divide an A4 piece of paper into two columns. List these competencies in the left-hand column and in the right-hand column write down your matching experiences in bullet point form. When considering the behaviours required in the position, look for alternatives. For example, you may have not worked as a Marketing Assistant, but even as a PA you may have had some input in the past into the way brand values are communicated to customers.

Writing your CV by focusing on critical incidents

You can often sharpen up the evidence in your CV by looking at "critical incidents" that have arisen in your last 12 months at work. A critical incident will often be one of the most exciting parts of the job because it represents a challenge or a time when you made a real difference. The situations may require high risk but also offer greater reward. The reason for taking the last 12 months is that, by considering the most recent experience, you have good recall of the detail of exactly what happened.

Use the Critical Incidents Worksheet to perform this exercise. Do not confine your review just to those incidents where things were all in your favour, but include times when problems ensued or your work was criticised. What did you learn from these "mistakes"? Focusing on real events helps avoid what one respondent in our survey described as "woolly" competency statements.

Critical Incidents Worksheet		
List critical incidents from each of your past jobs and what skills and/ or achievements were involved.		
Job	Critical Incident	Skill/Achievement
Example: Personal Assistant to MD	Had to contact and book keynote speaker while MD was off sick	Researching, communicating, influencing, persuading someone to move from no to yes, organising

How do I include competencies in my CV?

One HR manager in our survey complained that CVs often have "too much on competencies up front – I will make my own decisions based on the evidence presented. Often this is just generalisation – it needs to be targeted to the specific role".

Knowing what an employer is looking for, you need to think about the best way of offering matching evidence. Should this be in your CV? Sometimes this is best done in a covering letter. Occasionally you will be asked to write a separate statement matching your experience to the required competencies. If so, do this with care using this chapter as a guide. If you feel that the best way to sell yourself in the interview process is to spell out competencies in your CV, then consider the options.

Where competencies might appear in your CV	Advantages	Disadvantages
In the profile	Upfront and clear	This may make your profile too long
Job by job	It is easier for the reader to see where you used each competency	You may find competencies are repeated. Also, some of the key information may not appear on page 1
In the Achievements Section of page 1	Probably the favoured place – if you use an Achievements section. It's on page 1, and you can make clear links to evidence. You might choose to title each competency in bold	You may lose some of your strongest achievements from page 1 because they don't happen to match the list of competencies
As a separate list of competencies on page 1	You may decide to write a functional CV (see Chapter 5), using each competency as a section heading	You may find that this throws the structure of your CV out

Presenting a short list of competencies

What will probably happen is that you adapt the list of achievements you include on the first page of your CV so that it specifically picks up the sought-after competencies, e.g.:

> **Example Layout:**
>
> *Key Achievements and Competencies*
>
> • *Experienced team leader with a track record of **motivating teams** to achieve difficult targets*
>
> • *Well-developed on-my-feet communication skills, e.g. making quarterly presentations to demanding audiences of 100+ people*
>
> • *Responsibility for agreeing and managing budgets of up to £200K*
>
> • *Proven sales and negotiation skills demonstrated by 3 years of leading my team to win the Acme Inc UK sales award.*

Writing a competency statement

A strategy used by a number of employers now is to give you a list of anything between five and 20 competencies, and to ask you to write a written statement against each one. There will often be a prompt about how to structure your answer, and you may also be given a word limit. At other times there will be little or no information about how to structure your answers. In either case, the **7 Step Competency Flow Chart** will help you to formulate your evidence.

7 Step Competency Flow Chart

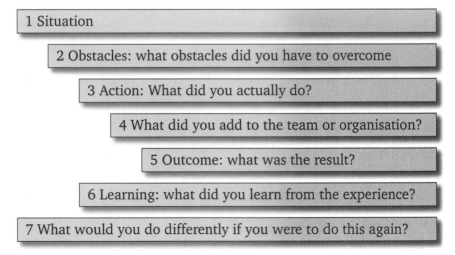

1 Situation

2 Obstacles: what obstacles did you have to overcome

3 Action: What did you actually do?

4 What did you add to the team or organisation?

5 Outcome: what was the result?

6 Learning: what did you learn from the experience?

7 What would you do differently if you were to do this again?

Using the 7 Step Competency Flow Chart

The flow chart above will help you to structure detailed written evidence of your competencies. (This will, of course, also help you to prepare good interview answers.)

- Start with the **situation** – a time when you used a skill or competency. You're looking for a good, sustainable example of where you used the competency. State that clearly.

- The next step is to look at **obstacles**, which requires you to ask yourself the spin-off question "What problems did I have to overcome?". These will vary enormously from one answer to another: lack of experience, perhaps, or time pressure or working with limited resources.

- Next, **action**. Once you have set out the obstacles clearly, spell out exactly what you did. This needs to be the main substance of your answer, and it needs to be expressed in the right language and at the right level. So, for example, stating "I asked my boss if I could" sounds like the competency is exercised at a very junior level, but stating "After negotiation I initiated a new project" sounds very different. Be very specific. Think through what you did, step by step, recording anything demanding or complex that relates to this specific competency.

- Remember to look carefully at tasks that were undertaken in a team. Selectors are trained to screen out "we did ..." statements, because they contain no evidence of your, distinctive contribution. If you worked as part of a team, what role did you take in the team? How did you get things done?

- Your written statement should include some kind of an **outcome**. What happened as a result of your actions? If you achieved a result that can be stated in measurable terms, do so. If the effect was on how people felt or what they experienced, get that across, e.g. "as a result of my intervention our biggest customer was kept on board and expressed a strong level of commitment to future business".

- The remainder of the evidence is about reflection. This means asking yourself, in general terms, what you learned from the experience, and what you would do differently if you were required to undertake this task again. You need not normally provide a huge amount on this topic in a written statement of your competencies, but the ability to recognise learning and to build on past experience is often found in the strongest candidates. Be prepared to talk about this in more depth at interview.

See below for an example of a written competency statement. As you can see, it uses the named competency as a sub-heading, and broadly follows the structure of the **7 Step Competency Flow Chart**.

Example of a completed Competency Statement

Leading and motivating teams

While studying I had to lead a team of six Business students giving a presentation about a recent workplace visit. We had to give a 15-minute PowerPoint presentation to the academic staff, and each of us had to make a contribution. The task was a challenge because two of the team had not enjoyed the visit and did not want to take part in the presentation. We had two unproductive meetings where not everyone was present. I got everyone together by providing free pizza and persuaded them to take a joint approach, which would present the positives and negatives of the experience. I then organised a schedule for preparing different parts of the presentation, designed the PowerPoint format and rehearsed each team member individually. I also organised the room booking and layout. The presentation went well and we all received a good mark, plus feedback that the team had worked well together and given a good range of feedback. Looking back on the experience I can see the importance of getting people to feel they are working together if you are going to make a public presentation, but I can also see how important it is to get to an agreed outcome quickly.

Evidence which worries a competence-based selector

Negative indicators are the kinds of evidence that recruiters are trained to spot in your evidence, which includes CVs and application forms.

The following (in written statements or at interview) will be taken as signs that you may not actually possess the competency at the right level:

✗ A statement like "what I usually do is …", "normally, I …" (or worse, "what we usually do …").

✗ Your opinion about what, in general terms, should be done (e.g. "I think it's important to …").

✗ Your speculation about what you would do in the future in a similar situation.

✗ A sentence beginning "What we did …" in which it is impossible to determine who actually performed the task. If you worked as part of a team, was your specific contribution?.

✗ Backing away from the right level, e.g. "I have managed people, but I wouldn't describe myself as a manager".

✗ Using words, in your interview or in your CV, which communicate a lack of complete engagement ("I was involved in …", "I participated in …").

Evidence that helps convince a competence-based selector

Recruiters undertaking competency-based selection are trained to spot the following as **positive indicators**, i.e. strong evidence that you possess the right competencies.

A selector will be looking for evidence from you (in written statements or at interview) that is:

✓ **From the past** – you describe a specific situation from your own experience.

✓ **Context** – you created a clear idea of the context: the people involved in the situation, the problems you had to overcome.

✓ **Individual** – your role in a team is crystal clear.

✓ **Unambiguous** – it is clear what you actually did and how you behaved.

✓ **Detailed Picture** – you have created a detailed story of what happened, what you did (planned, thought, said, improvised) as the situation unfolded.

✓ **Outcome** – the listener is clear about what happened as a result of your intervention.

✓ **Appropriate** – it matches the kind of behaviours an employer wants to see in the workplace.

✓ **Reflective** – you've clearly thought through your own actions and know how to learn from experiences.

✓ **Right Level** – you are demonstrating the competencies at the right level and standard for the job.

✓ **Motivation** – do you talk about your past work with the kind of energy that suggests you are motivated to use these competencies in the future?"

Here's an example of a checklist used by a recruitment consultant for short-listing candidates against competency-based criteria:

A RECRUITMENT CONSULTANT'S CHECKLIST OF COMPETENCIES

1. *What was the nature of the work the candidate has performed?*

2. *What were the key result areas in the candidate's last job?*

3. *What specific tasks did the candidate perform?*

4. *What competencies did the candidate require to complete these tasks?*

5. *What problems did the candidate deal with?*

6. *What is the candidate's attitude towards these tasks and problems?*

7. *What was the culture the candidate worked in?*

8. *How was the candidate's performance measured ?*

9. *How successful was the candidate in meeting or exceeding performance criteria?*

10. *What tangible evidence of success is there to back up the candidate's claims?*

11. *How did the candidate's performance match up with the rest of the team?*

12. *How flexible would the candidate be in transferring these skills to another type of work?*

COMPETENCY-BASED INTERVIEWS

The previous chapter has already looked in general terms at interviews. Competency-based interviews take a slightly different approach.

Past behaviours or future potential?

Behavioural questions are at the heart of competency-based selection procedures. This approach focuses far less on "biographical" information about you (e.g. your education, qualifications, work history, personality, and your past and present motivation) and puts far more emphasis on what you have done in the past, and how you did it. The core difference between biographical and competency-based interviews is set out below:

Biographical interviews focus on:	Competency-based interviews focus on:
Education	Skills
Qualifications	Achievements
Training	Attitudes
Work History	Values
Personal history	Knowledge put into practice
Family background	Observable behaviours
Availability	
Motivation	

The behavioural model contends that past performance is the best predictor of future performance ("can do" = "will do again"). In behavioural questioning, the interviewer asks candidates to supply evidence of past events that demonstrate all the elements that go into a competency: the skills you possess, the attitudes you demonstrate, the knowledge and values you bring to the job. You may equally be asked to submit this information in a statement, on an application form or in a covering letter.

As it is not always possible to find candidates with exactly matching experience, interviewers sometimes have to find parallel contexts. For this reason they sometimes ask about competencies used outside work. You may also be asked *"what would you do if ..."*. If the context suggested is something that you might have to face in the job, your interviewer will expect you to describe how you believe you would act in a particular situation.

Listening for the lead question

Typically you will hear a lead question in this kind of interview. This is designed to draw out a specific event from your past (i.e. looking for the "situation" part of the **7 Step Competency Flow Chart** outlined earlier). An interviewer should give you a fairly clear lead on this, e.g. "Tell me about a time when you had to work to conflicting deadlines ...". The lead question therefore clearly flags up which competency is being discussed, and steers you towards a particular context from your recent work experience.

Answering the lead question means bringing the right information out in the right order. The first thing to do is to be very clear about a specific occasion when you did something. You'll find that a timescale of a day or a week works best – anything you did over a longer period always sounds vague. Paint a clear picture ("The last time I led a difficult team was ...") and don't give too much background information. What a lot of candidates do here is say too much about the context, the organisation and its history, and how X connects with Y. This wastes valuable time because it says nothing about the competency.

Next, focus on what you did. Again, the **7 Step Competency Flow Chart** provides good prompts for putting together a structured answer. This time the emphasis needs to be on *matching your evidence exactly to the competency as described by the organisation*. If it's described in a document, prepare thoroughly in advance. If it's described by the interviewer, listen carefully (and ask for clarification if necessary), and deliver a response that is strictly focused on the competency *and all aspects of it*. For example, if you are asked to talk about the competency "working under pressure to strict deadlines" you will run the risk of exclusion if your example isn't about real pressure or about real deadlines. If you have to talk about "handling a difficult customer" then try to match your example against the kind of difficulty and the kind of customer experienced by this organisation.

Sometimes you will have to fish around in experience outside your conventional career to find evidence of competencies. Don't be put off by this – selectors are often instructed to take account of evidence from an individual's life outside paid work. However, if you do this, do some translating. So, for example, if you're asked to give an example of your competency as a fund-raiser and you can only do this by drawing on voluntary work, make sure the interviewer sees the relevance of the situation and skills. Don't undersell work you did on an unpaid basis. Too many people start by saying "the only time I have done this was outside work …" or "I've never done this for a living". Better to jump straight in with the context, the size of the problem and what you did, e.g. "working as a fund-raiser for our local environmental charity was a real challenge. We had no money in the bank and no contact list. What I first did was …".

Being probed

If you are a strong candidate, your well-structured, positive response to the lead question may do the trick. You should expect to be probed to at least two levels by a more experienced or astute recruiter. Your answers will be probed in a good competency-based interview. Probing is only difficult to handle if (a) you haven't really thought about the competency or (b) you haven't prepared enough evidence. If you hear any of the following it means you haven't been concrete or specific enough: *Can you give me an example? What did you do? What was the outcome?*

The recruiter may take other angles: What did you say? What did you feel about that? What was going through your mind? As the evidence is explored, you may also hear a question like "how would you do it differently if you did it again?".

Competencies at different levels

Probing will be used not only to find out whether you have actually done what you claim, but also to seek the **level** of the competency. How well do you perform the skill? How can you give objective evidence of a standard obtained (e.g. qualifications, training certificates, appraisal results)?

Dealing with personality questions

Not every interviewer knows the difference between personality traits and competencies. Often they will have in mind a certain personal characteristic that they feel is essential to the position. It may, or may not, be stated as part of a competency statement. So, for example, "decision making" is a skill, "decision making under pressure" is a competency (because it gives a sense of a context) and "making tough decisions under pressure" brings in aspects of tough-mindedness and resilience – aspects of personality. You should, therefore, plan to deal with questions that look in detail at personality traits – after all, you have probably already flagged up certain personal qualities in your CV profile. You will also have analysed the job in depth. Look through your analysis again. What personality traits do you think would be essential to success in the job? What characteristics would get in the way?

Questions on this topic can throw you. After all, you've spent a lot of time looking at skills and underlying knowledge in your CV, and probably taken your focus off the question of personality. Officially or unofficially this question screens out candidates. Traits can be viewed either as a positive or as a negative. Take, for example, in an advertising job being "creative" is a must, but not necessarily if you're going to work in quality inspection. Being "aggressive" may be the right quality in sales managers attacking new markets, but less so for someone whose job requires consultation with the community.

Making the most of preparation

This chapter has outlined the two key stages of the competency-based process: preparing your written evidence to help you get through a shortlisting process, and preparing for some fairly exacting interview questions. If you think the process looks obvious, don't mislead yourself: plenty of candidates fall at these very predictable hurdles through a failure to really understand what an employer is looking for, and how to package the evidence in a way that fits the process. Read instructions in this area with great care – failing to point out a piece of information or to provide the evidence in the precise way described are reasons why talented candidates fail to get through a competency-based selection process.

> *For a far more detailed discussion on competency-based selection processes see* Job Interviews: Top Answers to Tough Questions *by John Lees and Matthew DeLuca (McGraw-Hill, 2004).*

Covering Letters and Speculative Approaches

This chapter helps you to:

▌ Avoid classic errors in letters that get you rejected at the first hurdle

▌ Write a brief, focused cover letter that presents your CV in the best light

▌ Understand the structure of a good cover letter

▌ Explore the value of speculative approaches

"The two words 'information' and 'communication' are often used interchangeably, but they signify quite different things. Information is giving out; communication is getting through."

Sydney J Harris

COVERING LETTERS MATTER

No matter how brilliant your CV, it has to find its way to a decision maker. It will not arrive unannounced. If it's in response to an advertisement, you will need a covering letter to connect your personal information with the specific vacancy. Don't make the mistake made by thousands of job seekers every year and miss out on the basics. Quote the exact job title and reference, and make sure your letter is addressed to exactly the write person. Amazingly, this is a level of detail that escapes a significant proportion of covering letters.

The first mistake made when writing covering letters is to believe that the letter will sell you into the job. It won't. If you're lucky, it will simply persuade the reader to consider your CV. If it's a good letter, it will flag up three or four strong items in your CV worth considering.

The second mistake is to believe that you have to rehearse all the reasons why an employer should be interested in you. Again, this doesn't work. I have seen densely typed covering letters running for up to 3 pages. The detail never gets read, and people who write long covering letters rarely get the job – perhaps because they have already communicated their complete inability to edit information down to its bare essentials. When they hire people, busy managers are looking for staff with the ability to cut to the chase and present key information in abbreviated form. The function of a covering letter is a savoury appetiser before the main course.

On a very basic level, match your offer to the three or four obvious things stated in the job advertisement. You may think that the match is obvious, but do remember that your letter will be read by a busy recruiter. Recruitment specialists Robert Half offer the following advice on their website: "Mention three points that highlight your specific expertise in the area relevant to the job. Then mention three points explaining how your achievements show that you can add value to the company".

Classic errors in covering letters

Years of feedback from recruiters suggest to me that, despite all the advice available, people keep making the same mistakes when sending covering letters. Decision makers see too many letters that are:

- Standard letters which do not make strong connections to the job.

- Far too long.

- Full of extraneous information.

- Full of errors or misplaced humour.

Again, advice from Robert Half is useful: "Don't try to get your personality across in a covering letter. It's not really possible to do that without some kind of verbal communication. Save it for interview".

Reminders when you send a covering letter with your CV

The style and format of your letter should be simple. Use the same style and typeface as your CV. Your contact details should be clear.

What really matters is the content of your letter. If it's for an advertised position you don't need to refer to a target job or state what kind of role you are seeking. What does matter is that your letter says as much about the employer as it says about you. State why you are attracted to an employer. Use your letter as an opportunity to explain why your skills and experience might be useful, if this is not clear from your CV. Typically, what you will do is to pull out four or five things from the Job Description and, in the letter, carefully match them against your own experience. When you offer a brief range of selected achievements, make sure at least one of them is expressed in measurable terms. Make your letter interesting and readable, conveying energy and enthusiasm.

You may also want to use your letter to try to address any significant barriers. For example, if you do not have the relevant qualifications required, you will probably want to use a letter to argue the case that your experience provides you with the skills and know-how necessary to do the job.

Proof-read your covering letter for accuracy as diligently as you read your CV. Check, and double check, that you have spelled the name of the person you are writing to *absolutely correctly*. Keep your letter brief and to the point, another way of answering the question: *why you?* You will find that the "so what?" test from Chapter 8 works just as well here as in your CV profile. Don't make the mistake of thinking that the longer you argue your case, the better your chances of an interview. The opposite is almost certainly the case. If you can't write a one-page letter convincing someone to read your CV, how effective will your communication skills be in the job?

When it comes to submitting your CV online, recruiters often complain that they receive a covering letter that is in a separate file which takes time and trouble to open. It may be simpler to make your email message itself into a covering letter. See Chapter 14 for more tips. Even in the age of email there is a virtue in sending in a good-quality, unfolded CV with a smart-looking covering letter.

THINGS TO AVOID IN COVERING LETTERS

Don't:

- Use tired opening phrases like "This letter is written in response to" or "Please consider this application for the position of". Write something specific to the job or organisation instead.

- Oversell yourself with too much detail. Remember the letter's function is not to get you the job, but to get your CV read.

- Make mistakes in the way you address the letter. Ensure you have the correct name and job title. Don't write "Dear Sir/Madam" or "To whom it may concern". If it is addressed to a named individual (i.e. "Dear Mr Smith") it needs to end "Yours sincerely"; "Yours faithfully" should only be used when your letter begins "Dear Sir" or similar – which is best avoided because of its overformality.

- Repeat the exact words used in your CV to describe your achievements, or repeat extensive information from your CV – rephrase and summarise.

- Apologise in your letter, e.g. for the lack of a qualification or your age or referring to negative aspects such as why you left your last job.

- Be hesitant – phrases like "I think" and "perhaps" communicate lack of clarity.

- Seek an overcommitment. You can ask for a meeting, but don't ask for the job.

- Be over-assertive (e.g. "I will expect a call").

- Beg for an interview or offer special pleading (e.g. "please read this application carefully").

The structure of a good covering letter

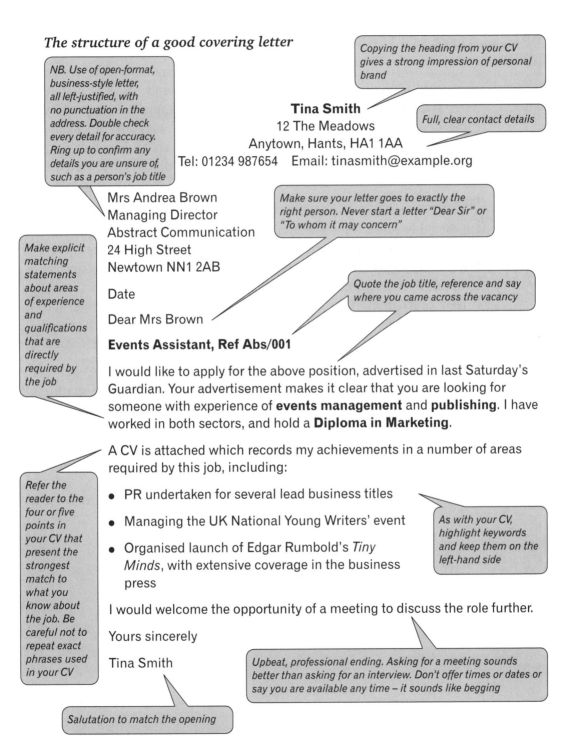

NB. Use of open-format, business-style letter, all left-justified, with no punctuation in the address. Double check every detail for accuracy. Ring up to confirm any details you are unsure of, such as a person's job title

Copying the heading from your CV gives a strong impression of personal brand

Full, clear contact details

Tina Smith
12 The Meadows
Anytown, Hants, HA1 1AA
Tel: 01234 987654   Email: tinasmith@example.org

Mrs Andrea Brown
Managing Director
Abstract Communication
24 High Street
Newtown NN1 2AB

Make sure your letter goes to exactly the right person. Never start a letter "Dear Sir" or "To whom it may concern"

Make explicit matching statements about areas of experience and qualifications that are directly required by the job

Date

Dear Mrs Brown

Quote the job title, reference and say where you came across the vacancy

Events Assistant, Ref Abs/001

I would like to apply for the above position, advertised in last Saturday's Guardian. Your advertisement makes it clear that you are looking for someone with experience of **events management** and **publishing**. I have worked in both sectors, and hold a **Diploma in Marketing**.

A CV is attached which records my achievements in a number of areas required by this job, including:

Refer the reader to the four or five points in your CV that present the strongest match to what you know about the job. Be careful not to repeat exact phrases used in your CV

- PR undertaken for several lead business titles

- Managing the UK National Young Writers' event

- Organised launch of Edgar Rumbold's *Tiny Minds*, with extensive coverage in the business press

As with your CV, highlight keywords and keep them on the left-hand side

I would welcome the opportunity of a meeting to discuss the role further.

Yours sincerely

Tina Smith

Upbeat, professional ending. Asking for a meeting sounds better than asking for an interview. Don't offer times or dates or say you are available any time – it sounds like begging

Salutation to match the opening

SPECULATIVE LETTERS

A speculative letter is a letter you send to an employer who is not currently advertising vacancies. The wrong kind of speculative letter is a waste of paper. The "spray and pray" approach adopted by some desperate job seekers means that your CV may end up in the waste-paper bin pretty quickly. Most letters that arrive like that very evidently have made little or no attempt to understand the needs of the organisation. Whether they arrive by post or email they are considered junk mail.

On the other hand, letters sent on a speculative basis to employers that are a reasonably good match to your skills and background are a very respectable instrument in the career changer's toolkit. Their effect is twofold: they may get you an interview with an employer but, even if they don't, they help to improve your visibility in the hidden job market. Even if they only lead to a conversation where you learn something about an employer and get to ask the question "who else should I be talking to?", the letter has worked.

Good, well-constructed speculative letters (to employers and to recruitment consultants) should be part of your job-search mix, but do ask yourself whether a letter is strictly necessary. Could you get the same result (or better) by speaking to a real person? Letters and CVs always work best as a back-up to a conversation, ideally one conducted face-to-face.

When a speculative letter might work

There are three times when speculative letters are highly effective:

1. When you have skills and experience which is in short supply. Employers will often create positions for skilled people just to get their talent in the organisation.

2. When you have carefully researched a target organisation, and you know enough about its needs and the way it hires to be able to write a convincing letter which you attach to your well-matched CV. This is going to be the result of an hour or more's active research.

3. Where you already have networked your way to a contact at an organisation and you are writing to confirm or add to what they already know about you.

How to find target organisations for your speculative letters

Approaches to organisations who are not advertising should be part of your multi-strategy job-search programme (see Chapter 11). Finding organisations is part of that activity.

There are several ways of finding organisations. The least productive way is by referring to directories. These tell you organisation names and how to find them, but little else. You will always get better results asking around – friends, colleagues, all kinds of contacts. You don't have to give full details of your target job – you can simply ask "who do you know that does X or Y?". As you gather names and recommendations, keep asking the question "who else should I be talking to?". In addition, look around you – drive round your local area and take note of organisations. Read your local press, taking note of any organisations named. Keep researching and digging, and always with one end in mind: the name and job title of a decision maker, and enough information about the organisation for you to make a credible application.

When a speculative letter probably won't work

If you are unclear about why you are applying, unsure about what there is in your experience that might interest a recruiter or if you just don't know enough about an organisation to write a convincing letter, then don't waste the stamp.

Similarly, you may discover that the organisation has a policy of ignoring all speculative letters because every application needs to be formally processed. Some organisations will only consider application forms, and only when specific posts are advertised. In this case you are best (a) applying for specific positions following the organisation's rules or (b) networking your way to a face-to-face conversation.

Problems with most speculative letters

As the reader of a speculative letter has no real motive for reading your letter, it matters that you get it right. Again, too many decision makers receive the wrong kind of approach:

- Letters that are entirely focused on you.

- Standard letters that do not relate to a specific job or employer.

- Sent to the wrong person.

- Write about a target job or an ideal organisation that is not relevant to this particular employer.

- Contain an unfocused message.

- Do not give a value reason for reading the CV.

A suggested format is set out below. Note that this follows most of the basics of the outline covering letter discussed earlier.

The structure of a good speculative letter to an employer

Tina Smith
12 The Meadows
Anytown, Hants, HA1 1AA
Tel: 01234 987654   Email: tinasmith@example.org

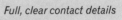 *Full, clear contact details*

Mr Andrew Smith
Technical
ABC Components Ltd
Main Drive
Newtown
NN1 2CD

Your letter must go direct to the top decision maker, not the HR department. Check the exact name and job title of the person you want to write to

Date

Dear Mr Smith

It was impressive to note in the industry press that ABC Components has won the ZZA contract.

At times like this effective controls on **purchasing** can make a huge difference. I am a **Senior Purchasing Professional** with experience in both pharmaceuticals and electronics.

Please find attached a CV which outlines my experience and achievements in a number of areas, including:

- Implementing a new e-purchasing function

- Achieving £12K savings over 36 months on a total spend of £200K

- Recruiting and motivating a key team of purchasing professionals.

Refer the reader to your CV. The only function of this letter is to get your CV read, and to get you an interview with a decision maker

I would welcome the opportunity of a meeting to discuss how I can contribute to your organisation.

Use bullet points to list a range of attractive and relevant achievements to persuade the reader to look at your CV

Yours sincerely

Tina Smith

Upbeat ending which asks for a meeting

Focus on something the reader should be proud of. A good letter also focuses on the employer, not you. Avoid beginning every paragraph with "I"

*Focus on the **needs** of the employer. Make it crystal clear what kind of role you want to fill, and throw in a summary of your relevant experience*

Speculative letters to recruitment consultants

A speculative letter is often a good way of getting your job-search story across to a busy recruitment consultant. Instead of referring to a specific organisation or role, this time the heading of your letter will be more general, e.g. "Management roles in the Health/Fitness Sector". Here again, you are dealing with a busy reader, so try to pull out the three or four key messages from your CV and (rephrasing them) include them in your covering letter.

Remember that recruitment consultants are relationship-driven, not paper-driven, so you are far more likely to make a connection if you can speak to a recruiter. The way to do this is often to spot the agencies who are regularly advertising jobs in your chosen sector. Find the individual consultants who are handling specific roles. Administrators and secretaries will discourage you from speaking to them, but you will often get through if you need to ask a detailed or technical question about the role advertised. Then state *very briefly* what you are looking for, and what you have to offer. Afterwards send in your CV with a strong covering letter and phone up again in a couple of days' time to ensure the CV has been received, and ideally to build on the relationship.

Example speculative letter to a recruitment consultant

Tina Smith
12 The Meadows
Anytown, Hants, HA1 1AA
Tel: 01234 987654   Email: tinasmith@example.org

Full, clear contact details

Ms Anita Patel
Senior Consultant
AAA Staffing
212 The Mews
Newtown
NN1 2BQ

Send the letter to a named consultant. Check the exact name and job title

Date

Use a general heading that specifies role (sector, if important) and location

Beginning with a telephone call establishes a relationship and suggests reasons why the reader might want to consider your CV

Be very specific about your role, function, key skills and relevant qualifications

Dear Ms Patel

Accounting Technician Roles in central Newtown

It was good to speak to you this morning and to look at your very helpful website. I am ready to move to a new permanent position.

I am a **qualified Accounting Technician** with experience in both the service sector (Uniting Utilities) and manufacturing (AA Biscuits).

Please find attached a CV which outlines my experience and achievements, including the following:

Refer the reader to your CV. This letter's function is to get the recruiter to understand what you are looking for and to take the next step, which might include a meeting

- Experience of shared service accounting functions

- Purchase and Sales ledger experience

- Measurable improvements in debt recovery

- Familiarity with a broad range of accounting software.

Use bullet points to list a general range of relevant achievements which a recruiter will find useful when placing you

I would welcome the opportunity of a meeting to discuss my CV and potential roles.

Yours sincerely

Ask for a meeting. A recruiter is far more likely to recommend you if he/she gets to know you in person

Tina Smith

Think about perspective

Before you post off or email your letter, read it from the perspective of a busy recruiter, manager or HR specialist. You may have spent hours crafting the exact words you want to use, filling out your letter with lots of detail, but your letter will be skim-read – in seconds. Is it clear why you are writing, and what you hope your letter will achieve? Can it be said in less words? Are you trying to make too many points?

Whatever the purpose of the letter, *don't make it entirely about you*. Too many covering and speculative letters are written entirely from the applicant's point of view. Every paragraph, every sentence, begins with the word "I". A far better discipline is to try to start at least some paragraphs with something else. Try the word "your" (e.g. "Your advertisement", "Your website", etc.).

Wherever your letter is going, say at least one thing about the organisation to whom the letter is addressed. If you are writing a covering letter in application for a job, or a speculative letter, refer to something you have noticed about your target organisation – something new, something relevant, something that has attracted you. Employers spend a great deal of money trying to get noticed, so telling them that their budget was well spent is not a bad move. If you're writing a speculative letter where there is no advertised vacancy, say what it was that attracted you in the first place, otherwise it sounds like your only reason for writing is that you want a job. If you're writing a speculative letter to a recruitment consultant, say how you have come across them (sometimes it helps to mention an organisation or senior manager who recommended this particular agency).

Whatever you do, and whoever you write to, try to give a *value reason* for writing – a good reason why someone should read your speculative letter. This is, ultimately, going to be connected to the idea that bringing your skills on board is going to provide tangible benefits.

Using Your CV Online

This chapter helps you to:

I Investigate the usefulness of Internet job sites

I Prepare a CV for it to be read electronically

I Write a CV to emphasise keywords

I Be careful about confidential information online

I Begin to start searching for jobs

"The modern human communicates better with his mouse than with his mouth."

Paul Carvel

IS AN ONLINE JOB SEARCH WORTHWHILE?

Employers are increasingly using online recruitment methods. In its *Recruitment, Retention and Turnover Survey Report 2006*, the Chartered Institute of Personnel & Development noted that over 70% of organisations say they are advertising jobs on their own corporate websites and using online applications. Other recent trends in online recruitment are equally interesting: online job seekers continue to become more senior. According to the National Online Recruitment Audience Survey (NORAS), the average salary sought by the online job seeker rose from £22,700 in 2002 to £34,600 in 2006. Job seekers are becoming more loyal to particular websites, which now handle jobs right up to the most senior level.

The services offered by online job sites vary considerably, but tend to encompass one or more of the following:

1. A **searchable jobs database** – candidates submit their CVs for jobs that interest them.

2. A **client-focused database** service – candidates register their details, but you only hear about a job when a consultant thinks you are a good match to the requirements of the job.

3. **Recruitment advertisements** – which will include anonymous advertisements, general advertising from agencies and advertisements that name the final employer.

A word of warning: don't spend too much time using the Internet. It is a fantastic research tool, but a less than perfect job-search tool. Because it feels like hard work loading your CV and searching sites, it feels like a productive activity. It is productive, but far less so than other job-search methods, particularly networking. The danger is that you get stuck behind a computer screen and you are not making useful relationships. One rule of thumb used by US career coaches is "only use your computer outside working hours" – during normal hours of work your time is spent far more productively if you are talking to real people.

HOW WILL YOUR CV BE CONVERTED?

There are many ways your CV might be converted into electronic format:

- Your paper CV is scanned by a recruiter.

- You send your CV as an email attachment.

- You submit your CV to a web-based system.

Those organisations that handle CVs in larger quantities (including major employers and recruitment consultancies) often prefer electronic CVs because of the saving in cost and time. It is claimed that CV management systems search 30,000 CVs in as little as 6 seconds. Such a system is generally designed to pick out information from a CV in a way that the human eye cannot readily do.

SHOULD I WRITE A DIFFERENT VERSION FOR ONLINE USE?

There are many websites that advise you to develop a CV for electronic use that is different from your conventional document.

The reality is that most of the time all that you will need to do is alter the format for the Internet. For some career changers all that needs to be done is to ensure that your well-prepared CV is reformatted so that it can be read electronically. However, if you suspect that you will need to use different or more keywords if your CV is read by a computer, you may need to rethink content as well.

SUBMITTING YOUR CV BY EMAIL

Most of the time your CV will be transferred electronically it will be sent as an email attachment. Many recruitment consultants ask you to submit your CV this way. Remember that the way it prints off on your printer will not necessarily be the same as the printer used by the consultant – which is why it's often a good idea to keep formatting in your CV simple, and make sure that you don't have any lines that might be printed on the wrong page (there is a "keep with next" paragraphing format function in Word you can use to prevent this happening). If in doubt, submit a paper copy as well.

PREPARING YOUR CV IF YOU KNOW IT WILL BE SCANNED

CVs are scanned for keywords. At one stage this was only done for IT workers (where a search for the name of a particularly computer program could pick out those with relevant experience). Sometimes employers choose keywords for exclusion. More commonly they will use a piece of software to screen out CVs that do not include particular words.

If you are creating a CV to be read by a computer think carefully about including the right keywords. Some systems look for action verbs (e.g. "developed," "initiated" and "achieved" – the same kind of language that would attract a human reader. However, an automated system is more likely to look for nouns and phrases relevant to the sector. Examples of keywords will include:

- **Job Titles** (e.g. Designer, Project Manager, Sales Manager).

- **Software Applications** (Java, Unix, C++, CAD, MS Project, Photoshop, Dreamweaver).

- **Key Technical Words, Phrases, Acronyms** (e.g. Six Sigma, Prince2, Direct Mail, TQM).

- **Industry-specific phases** (e.g. Quality Management, Pharmaceuticals, Product Launch, Market Research, Performance Testing, Public Relations).

It's vital to remember that a computer is unable to search intelligently for information or interpret your text – it will only look for the keywords entered by the user. As a result, many online job sites recommend that you include as many keywords as possible. It's almost exactly like designing a website so that it will be picked up by search engines: try to think of the different words that a recruiter might be looking for, and include obvious variations (e.g. type "TQM" and also "Total Quality Management").

If you know that your CV is going to be read electronically, formatting is the second problem on your hit list. When a computer scans a CV into its database, some kinds of formatting will cause problems. Almost all websites asking you to submit a CV will ask you to send a simple CV with minimum formatting.

THINGS TO AVOID IF YOUR CV WILL BE SCANNED

- Do not fold your CV if you send it by post. Send it flat or in a stiff envelope, and make sure it is clearly printed on clean, white paper.

- Do not include bullet points – some computers apparently interpret bullets as the letter 'o', which would make your information look misspelled.

- Do not include any information in tables or boxes.

- Do not use underlining, bold text or italics, and do not mix font sizes and styles.

- Remove any other design features, including printed lines.

- Do not use columns or boxes.

- Avoid using tabs.

FORMATTING THAT HELPS IF YOUR CV WILL BE SCANNED

- Put your name at the top of the page, on a line by itself. Make sure the name on your CV matches the name you use when registering or on emails.

- Use a "sans serif" typeface for the plainest image for each letter (examples of sans serif fonts are Arial, Verdana or Tahoma).

- Leave plenty of space between different sections of the CV to make sure they don't run into each other.

- Use headings in capital letters to title new sections.

- When including a telephone number use dashes to separate groups of numbers (do not use brackets which can be misread).

USING YOUR INTERNET-READY CV TO COMPLETE ONLINE APPLICATION FORMS

The final way that your CV might become electronic data is if you load parts of it onto a Job Site on the Internet that asks you to complete an online application form. Sometimes this is referred to as an online CV – the difference is that you are required to fit information into boxes provided on screen, rather than sending in a complete document.

The best way is to begin with a plain text version of your CV – i.e. the kind of CV you would use to submit online. You can open this document on screen and then cut and paste into online forms. Another way is to break your CV up into different sections (e.g. "Key Skills", "Training", "Qualifications") and create a plain text file in your word-processing software for each topic.

If you find that you are frequently submitting other kinds of information in online applications, once again it's worth pre-preparing text files. This is particularly useful when providing evidence of achievements or examples of when you have demonstrated specific competencies.

WHY SHOULD I USE MY CV ON THE INTERNET?

There are several reasons why you should submit your CV electronically. First, it's the fastest way of submitting a document. Candidates sometimes submit a CV online, have a telephone interview and receive a job offer during the course of a single day Furthermore, you have access to vacancies 24 hours a day, 7 days a week. Email can be copied, forwarded, distributed, copied or printed quickly and easily – it is far more flexible than a faxed document.

PREPARING A "PLAIN TEXT" CV

Most word processors and CV-writing programs will let you save a file as a "text only" document. Before saving in this format, it is worth taking an intermediate step. Make a working copy of your carefully formatted document, and in this copy (save your original carefully) remove all non-text effects such as bullet points as well as lines or boxes. Next, ensure that you take out all text effects, such as bold type or italics. This new file, even if saved in Word or a similar package, may be suitable for uploading. You can, however, also save the file as a text-only document if this is required.

When you have created a text-only file (this will probably have a ".txt" suffix) edit it carefully so that each section is clearly separated. Instead of bullet points you can use asterisks or dashes. You can also indent using character spaces if you want some lines to stand out. You may need to turn off the Autoformatting function in Word. When you have a text-only CV, it is a good idea to email it to yourself or to a friend to see how it looks.

CONFIDENTIALITY

Remember that, once it is posted, your CV is potentially a public document. Although some databanks offer confidentiality, the reality is that you cannot control who has access to your CV once it is online. Reputable online sites take candidate information very seriously, but always consider the credentials of any site carefully. A confidentiality or privacy policy should include information on where your information will be sent, whether your permission is required before it is sent on to companies, whether the site will send information to third parties and how long your information will stay available to others.

Be particularly careful about including personal details on an online CV. Often it is unwise to include your home address and telephone number. It's generally a good idea to use your email address as the sole method of contacting you and put "Contact details unavailable on public version" on your online CV.

Also, you should be aware that other countries have different equal opportunity policies and identifying age, sex or gender, ethnic background and family circumstances in your CV or application form may not be acceptable. You should never send a photograph (unless it is required specifically for the job, e.g. theatre or modelling), as this again would probably contravene an equal opportunity policy.

Identity theft is a growing problem, and one way for personal information to be abused is through online CV banks. Genuine employers or agencies will not ask for National Insurance numbers, or bank or credit card details. Do not disclose personal information not relevant to the job you are applying for, e.g. marital status, mother's maiden name. Be careful of unrealistic promises of work and never agree to pay for an interview or an introduction to an employer.

SHOULD I PAY TO LOAD MY CV ONLINE?

There are so many free sites available now that you should not consider any site that charges you just to submit a CV. It is against the law for a recruitment agency to charge you to help find you a job. Some job sites offer "premium" and other charged services, but check any site carefully that proposes to charge you simply to upload your CV. Equally, avoid sites that attempt to charge you to update or revise your CV.

SEARCHING THE WEB

A search engine can help you find recruitment websites (sometimes known as Job Boards) or may take you directly to the website of an organisation that has its own vacancies. However, typing individual words into search engines generates too many responses. If you type the word "jobs" into Google you will produce over 600 million listed web pages. The simple addition of selecting "pages from the UK" reduces this to 61 million, but this is, again, far too many. Determine your key search criteria in advance – location, job role, skills, salary, technical expertise. Use these keywords to narrow the vacancies down to a manageable number.

Learn how different search engines work. With Google, listing several words will return pages with these words anywhere in the text. Putting a phrase in quotation marks lists just those pages that contain exactly that phrase. Putting a minus sign before a search term will exclude pages that contain that word. Putting a plus sign before a search term will exclude pages that do not contain that word (common words such as "a" and "the" are removed by search engines from the search). Remember that different words can be used to describe the same role – so try different variations of words and phrases.

If you are trying to find out information about particular occupations you may not want to go directly to job boards. Sites such as www.prospects.ac.uk provide a lot of general information about career paths, entry routes and professional bodies you can contact. These bodies often have a great deal of useful careers-related information on their websites.

Finally, don't neglect websites operated by employers as well. They will be vital if you are preparing a speculative letter or applying for a specific job.

Appendix: Recommended Websites

www.bbc.co.uk/skillswise/words/writing/	General tips on writing well
www.askoxford.com/betterwriting	Tips on writing crisper, clearer English
www.cv-library.co.uk/	CV-creating website
www.europeanresources.co.uk/jobseekers/writingcvs.html	General CV advice
www.careers.manchester.ac.uk/getting/cvs/	Step-by-step guide to writing a CV from the University of Manchester Careers Service
www.alec.co.uk/cvtips/index.htm	Broad range of CV advice with plenty of example CVs
www.cvservices.net	CV advice and guidance. The site offers appraisal of CVs
http://news.bbc.co.uk/1/hi/business/2950896.stm	CV-writing tips from the BBC

www.timesonline.co.uk/tol/life_and_style/ career_and_jobs/graduate_management/ article1291098.ece	Useful tips
www.businessballs.com/curriculum.htm	A huge range of free CV tips
www.badenochandclark.com/Content_ Candidates/CM_cv.asp	Advice from a recruitment consultancy
www.givemeajob.co.uk	A site for you to post your CV and gives advice on job search and employers
www.capemed.com/reg.html	How to write a CV for a health sector job in the UK
www.workthing.co.uk/career-advice/cv-writing/	CV-writing advice from the Guardian's website
http://content.monster.co.uk/9334_en-GB_ p1.asp	Ten things recruiters hate to see in CVs
www.bradleycvs.co.uk/cv-writing-tips/ cv-summary.htm	Tips on writing a profile
www.uknec.org.uk	Sites that help you to write a CV in Europass format
http://europass.cedefop.europa.eu/europass/ home	
www.iagora.com/iwork/resumes	For help writing a CV for the USA, France, Germany, Spain and Sweden
www.eurograduate.com	Advice on presenting a CV for a wide range of European countries
www.jobweb.com/resources	Suggestions for writing a CV for Japan and Canada

www2.warwick.ac.uk/services/personnel/jobsintro/apply/cv/	How to write an academic CV
www.kent.ac.uk/careers/cv/PostgradCV.htm	Writing a postgraduate CV
www.accreditedqualifications.org.uk/	Government site giving full information about school-based qualifications
www.ucas.com	Information about university courses and degrees
www.accreditedqualifications.org.uk/	A site that allows you to search a qualifications database
http://content.monster.co.uk/job_hunting	Monster.co.uk's guide to online job search
www.philb.com/searchindex.htm	Tips for searching the Internet
www.pearsoned.co.uk/bookshop/minds/gradcareers/internet.htm	Job searching using the internet
www.support4learning.org.uk/jobsearch/cover_letters_for_careers_and_jobsearch.cfm	List of different job sites that will help you to write covering letters aimed at UK employers
http://content.monster.co.uk/6459_en_p1.asp	Ten things to avoid in covering letters
www.workthing.com/career-advice/cv-writing/under_judges.html	Advice on writing strong covering letters
www.get.hobsons.co.uk/advice/interviews_selection	Advice on selection centres
www.interimmanagement.uk.com	Information about working as an Interim Manager

Index

How To Get A Job You'll Love
A practical guide to unlocking your talents and finding your ideal career

John Lees

"A jewel of a book to help even the most luckless and career-panicked person."
Management Today

"Offers a fresh look at career planning."
The Guardian

"Thought-provoking, stimulating and a pleasure to read."
People Management

9780077114718
Paperback £12.99

How to Get a Job You'll Love is now in its fourth (2007/08) edition and is proving to be one of the most popular careers titles by a British author. It takes a uniquely creative look at career planning, helping you to discover your hidden skills, what really interests you in life, and your career "hot buttons". By tapping into your hidden talents it will help you to identify the kind of career you really want.

Learn more. Do more.

www.mcgraw-hill.co.uk

Job Interviews: top answers to tough questions

Matthew J Deluca & John Lees

9780077107048
Paperback £8.99

Job Interviews: Top Answers to Tough Questions will put you streets ahead of the competition, helping you think through hundreds of tough questions and respond with total confidence. Whether you are a first time job hunter or going for your dream promotion, this is your comprehensive toolkit for dealing with awkward, probing, personality and competency based interview questions.

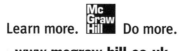

Learn more. Do more.

www.mcgraw-hill.co.uk

Take Control Of Your Career
Practical steps to improve your working future

John Lees

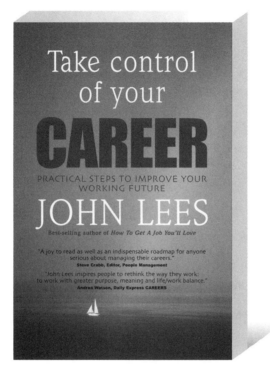

"Work has come to mean a lot more than a career ladder and a salary, and nobody understands that better than John Lees."

Psychologies

9780077109677
Paperback £12.99

Take Control of Your Career is a practical guide to developing the best career strategy for you. Whether you want to take your next step up the career ladder, move to a more interesting job or devote more energy to learning and living, this book gives you the tools and techniques to achieve your goals.

A Manager's Guide to
Self Development, 5th edition

Mike Pedler, John Burgoyne, Tom Boydell

9780077114701
Paperback £19.99

A Manager's Guide to Self Development has become the indispensable guide for building management skills. Now in its fifth edition the book details a self-development programme aimed at helping readers improve their managerial performance, advance their careers and realise their full potential.

Learn more. **Mc Graw Hill** Do more.

www.mcgraw-hill.co.uk